CYBORGS, GENES AND TINY MACHINES

For Sidney. The future of medicine is FANTASTIC, just like you are!

Published in 2023 by Welbeck Children's
An Imprint of Welbeck Children's Limited,
part of the Welbeck Publishing Group
Offices in: London - 20 Mortimer Street, London W1T 3JW
& Sydney - Level 17, 207 Kent St, Sydney NSW 2000 Australia
www.welbeckpublishing.com

Design and layout © Welbeck Children's Limited 2023
Text copyright © 2023 Paul Ian Cross
Published by arrangement with Speckled Pen Limited
Illustration © Welbeck Publishing Limited,
part of Welbeck Publishing Group

Writer: Paul Ian Cross, PhD
Illustrator: Steve Brown
Designer: Paul Southcombe
Design Manager: Matt Drew
Editorial Manager: Joff Brown
Production: Melanie Robertson

ISBN: 978 1 78312 986 7

A CIP catalogue record for this book is available from the British Library.

Printed in the UK

10 9 8 7 6 5 4 3 2 1

Paul Ian Cross, PhD

CYBORGS, GENES
AND TINY MACHINES

Illustrated by Steve Brown

The
MINDBLOWING
FUTURE of
MEDICINE!

WELBECK

Contents

CHAPTER 1

MARVELLOUS MEDICINE

The **HUMAN BODY** is a **MARVEL** of **EVOLUTION**. A perfectly adapted machine, developed over millions of years of trial and error.

But even the best equipment can break down.

Fortunately, over thousands of years, humanity has discovered incredible ways of understanding, treating and preventing illness.

So before we zoom into the future, let's look at the **MARVELLOUS WORLD** of **MEDICINE!**

Sometimes, we get injured or become unwell. We may cut our finger or catch a cold. Or something more serious may happen, like when someone's genetic make-up makes them vulnerable to a disease.

Fortunately, there are trained medical staff on hand to help. They have invested years of their life – sometimes as many as **TWELVE** years! – into training, just to make sure that we all stay fit and healthy.

And other scientists are working all the time to explore the future of medicine – to anticipate new diseases and prepare for them, or to improve technology and invent new treatments.

What is medicine?

Most people think of medicine as a cough mixture, or an inhaler for asthma from the chemist. But medicine is actually a whole science!

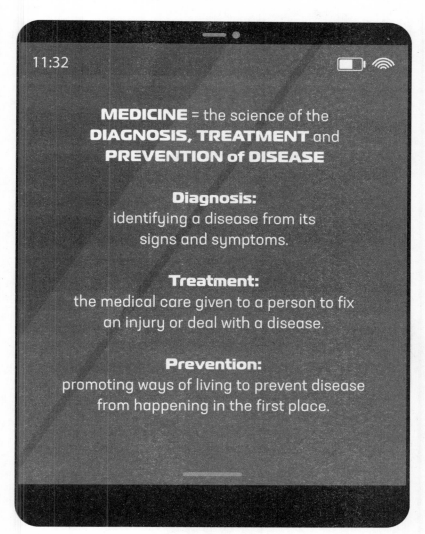

11:32

MEDICINE = the science of the
DIAGNOSIS, TREATMENT and
PREVENTION of DISEASE

Diagnosis:
identifying a disease from its
signs and symptoms.

Treatment:
the medical care given to a person to fix
an injury or deal with a disease.

Prevention:
promoting ways of living to prevent disease
from happening in the first place.

Compared to our ancestors, we now enjoy longer and healthier lives - mainly due to the medical advances of the past 200 years. These advances include everything from artificial organs to bionic limbs, and even changing people's genes. We're living in amazing times.

Our understanding of how the human body works and how disease happens continues to expand. Advanced technologies are also changing how doctors diagnose, treat and manage all types of conditions.

What new terrific tech? Well, things like:

O **Incredible IMAGING SYSTEMS,** used to look inside our brilliant bodies and spot disease earlier

O **Super surgical DEVICES** like pacemakers, helping someone's heart to work properly

O **Awesome APPS** that monitor our heart rate and blood pressure

The science of modern medicine is only going to grow **BIGGER**. And **BETTER**. Where will all this knowledge and technology lead us?

In this book you'll learn about the very latest science...

O   How to build a cyborg

O   Geniuses who are changing people's genes

O   Remarkable robotics

O   Technological triumphs of tiny machines

...and so
much more!

Prepare to be
wowed by wearable
technology and
amazed by the
awesomeness of AI!
Your **FUTURE**
is going to be
FANTASTIC! *

*Mainly because you're reading
this book, but also thanks to
the marvels of medicine!

Hooray for history

To explore the future, we need to understand our past. Human medicine has been happening for thousands of years. Where did it all start? According to the famous anthropologist Dr Margaret Mead, it coincided with the...

DAWN OF HUMAN CIVILISATION!

Awesome Anthropology

Anthropologists are scientists who study humankind. They look at humans throughout time and:

○ Find out how people's bones, diet and health changed

○ Learn how ancient cultures and civilisations developed and piece together ancient languages

○ Study artifacts, like spears and knives, to see how they were used for hunting

○ Trace our evolution from fossils

○ Investigate how we communicate across different communities

○ Look at how we use social media to share knowledge

HELPING ANOTHER THROUGH **DIFFICULTY** IS WHERE **CIVILISATION** STARTS.

Anthropologist Margaret Mead

For Margaret, the clue to the dawn of human civilisation lay in a 15,000-year-old skeleton.

What was so special about this skeleton? Well, the person who died 15,000 years ago had broken their thigh bone (femur) at some point in their life. Humans probably broke bones all the time, but in this case, after the bone had broken... it was allowed to heal.

You see, when a bone heals it looks different to how it did before. Why does a healed bone matter?

Because in the wild if an animal breaks its leg it usually doesn't last very long. It wouldn't be able to find food or water or escape from predators. It would die of starvation, thirst or get eaten by something with big teeth.

The healed bone showed something remarkable. Somebody – perhaps a relative or friend – cared for this person until they were better. It was in this moment that medicine was invented. Possibly!

Medical milestones

2500 BC   The healing practice of acupuncture is developed in China.

500 BC   The Sushruta Samhita – one of the largest medical texts of the time – is made in India.

c460 BC   Hippocrates is born in Ancient Greece. He goes on to become a famous physician and rejects the idea that disease is caused by magic!

1025   The Canon of Medicine was completed by Ibn Sina, a Persian physician and philosopher, who wrote hundreds of medical and scientific texts.

1300   Spectacles are mentioned for the first time in historical texts around this time.

1590   The first microscope is developed.

1665   Robert Hooke describes a 'cell' for the first time.

1865   Louis Pasteur describes how infectious diseases can spread through the air.

1895   The first X-ray images are created.

20TH CENTURY

1928 Sir Alexander Fleming discovers penicillin, an antibiotic.

1933 The electron microscope is invented.

1953 Rosalind Franklin, Maurice Wilkins, James Watson and Francis Crick show how Deoxyribonucleic Acid (DNA) is shaped like a twisted ladder.

1954 First successful kidney transplant.

1967 First successful heart transplant.

1980 The World Health Organisation declares that smallpox has been eradicated, thanks to vaccines!

1996 BAAAAA! The first cloned sheep, Dolly, is born in Scotland.

2003   The Human Genome Project is completed —
          mapping out all our genes.

2008   Gene therapy is used to correct faulty genes
          in patients with an immune disease.

2010   The first operation by a robotic surgeon is
          performed in Canada.

2013   Stem cells are used to grow tiny livers
          in a Japanese lab.

2013   Scientists use CRISPR — a way of editing DNA
          — in mammalian cells for the first time.

2020   mRNA vaccines are rapidly developed during
          the COVID-19 pandemic.

2022   A pig's heart is transplanted into a human for
          the first time. It's true! I'm not telling porkies!

Where in the world?

Where did these medical milestones happen?

1 Tiny livers grown using stem cells

2 Acupuncture developed

3 Dolly the sheep cloned

4 First robotic operation

5 Publication of the Sushruta Samhita

a Canada

b China

c India

d Scotland

e Japan

Turn the page upside down to see the answers!

17

Answers: 1e, 2b, 3d, 4a, 5c

The DNA relay race!

Future medicine can only happen if scientists work **TOGETHER** – sometimes over decades. Here's how three different sets of scientists passed the baton to each other, helping discover the wonders of DNA over the course of eighty years.

First Leg

DNA was first discovered by Swiss researcher Friedrich Miescher in 1869. As a young man he had typhoid fever, which left him hearing-impaired, but this didn't stop his determination to become a chemist.

START

Second Leg

Then, in the early 1950s, Dr Rosalind Franklin and Dr Maurice Wilkins did their own research based on Miescher's work. They studied DNA using X-rays. Rosalind created a photo that showed that DNA is shaped like a twisted ladder, called a double helix.

Third Leg

Rosalind's incredible image helped Dr James Watson and Dr Francis Crick to develop a model of how DNA works. Watson and Crick's paper, published in the journal Nature in 1953, laid the groundwork for understanding DNA.

Relay Race WON!

The Perfect Prize

Together with Maurice Wilkins, Watson and Crick were awarded the 1962 Nobel Prize in Physiology and Medicine for their DNA discoveries. Rosalind would have also been recognised, but unfortunately, she had passed away from ovarian cancer by this time. Nobel prizes are only awarded to living people and not after death. But scientists today recognise that Rosalind's achievements were fundamental to the discovery of DNA.

Details about disease

Humans, animals and plants all get diseases. But wait...
what is disease, anyway? And what causes it?
Well, a disease is when harmful changes occur inside
an organism, away from what is considered healthy
and normal. These changes can be related to the
body's structure or how the body works. They are
normally picked up because a person experiences
signs and symptoms (but not always). A disease is not
the same as an injury.

The study of disease is called PATHOLOGY.

1. It involves finding the cause of the disease
   (aetiology) and...

2. Understanding the ways in which
   the disease develops (pathogenesis).

Not so cute!

Diseases can be acute or chronic.

Acute

Acute doesn't refer to the cute bunny you saw in the pet shop. In medicine, acute means the rapid appearance of disease. It can often be serious. For example:

O Heart attacks are when a blood clot or other blockage stops blood flow to part of the heart.

O Strokes happen where blood supply to part of the brain is cut off.

These may sound scary, but thankfully doctors, nurses and scientists have been working for years to develop new treatments to help!

Chronic

These last for an extended time, often months or years. For example:

O Arthritis: the 'wear and tear' of joints such as the knees, hips and wrists.

O Cancer: the uncontrollable growth of abnormal cells in the body.

Injury time

An injury is when something in the body is broken or damaged. Injuries happen due to **impact with someone or an object**, **sudden movement**, or due to our **environment** – for example, heat causes dehydration, while cold causes hypothermia.

Types of injuries include:

Fractures: when bones break. **SNAP!**

Dislocations: when bones are wrenched out of a joint. **OUCH!**

Sprains: when ligaments are stretched or torn. **OOPS!**

Strains: when a muscle or tendon is overstretched or torn. **YIKES!**

Bruises: when an impact causes blood vessels to burst under the skin. **BUMP!**

Cuts: when a sharp object impacts the skin, breaking the surface. **RIIIIIIP!**

Grazes and blisters: when wounds are caused by rubbing or friction. **SCRATCH!**

But thanks to science, one day it may be possible to...

ABOLISH ALL INJURY and
PUT A SQUEEZE ON DISEASE for good!

Let's get personal!

Once upon a time, doctors used the same treatments for everybody. They'd use the same chemotherapy drugs to treat a type of cancer, or they'd give people the same set of medicines for their high blood pressure. But, more recently, we've discovered that **ONE SIZE DOES NOT FIT ALL**. What works for one person may not work for another.

Ours is a **NEW ERA** of **HEALTHCARE.** The era of **PERSONALISED MEDICINE**. This allows treatments to be tailored to each person, which means it is improving the way we treat illness.

How do scientists do this? By understanding our DNA, of course!

Quite frankly, it's **GENE-IUS**.

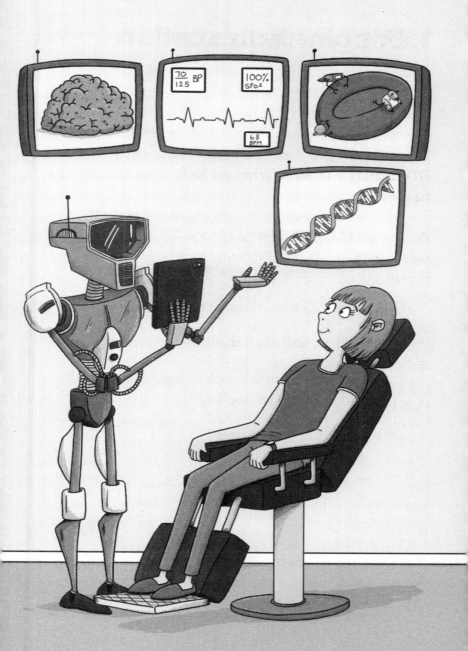

Imagination station

Consider this curious question and let your imagination run wild!

As scientists learn more about our DNA, we may eventually put a stop to all diseases. Maybe, one day, NO ONE would ever get sick.

Why not try writing a story about a world with NO MORE DISEASE!

O What would it mean for the world?

O What if old people never got ill or weak?

O Would we still need doctors and hospitals?

O How could we make sure everyone around the world was always healthy?

The answers are up to you!

CHAPTER 2

SMALL SCIENCE

When you look at the future of medicine, it gets **SMALLER** and smaller and smaller!

Why? Because small science is **BIG** science. It helps us get to the bottom of things. And that's why small ideas build the future.

When we go **MINIATURE**, we find clever ways to help the world. This might be through editing our genes, delivering medicines in new ways, or by using medical robots that could swim through our blood!

So don't think big, think small!
It's time to SHRINK **SCIENCE**!

Famous scientist Albert Einstein

Research has shown that to really understand how our bodies work and how disease happens, we need to study cells

UP CLOSE.

(Even closer than that!)

 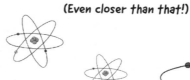 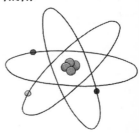

It could 'atom' to you!

Science has proved that there is more going on inside our cells than we could ever imagine. Not long ago, the ability to make changes to our cells only existed in science fiction books and films. Now, scientists can make changes to our cells... and much smaller things, down to the level of atoms.

Q: Why can't you trust atoms?

A: Because they 'make up' everything!

The Truth Is Out There

Science fiction includes any imagined story based around advances in science and technology that are yet to happen. These can involve space, robots and even life on other planets. That's right... aliens! A lot of modern science was predicted in science fiction, so perhaps it can tell us about our future too.

So, when we say 'science', what do we really mean? It breaks down into three parts...

BIOLOGY is the study of **living organisms**.

CHEMISTRY is the study of **matter** (physical stuff).

PHYSICS is the study of **matter AND energy**, such as heat, light, sound, electricity, magnetism and how atoms are made up.

Because everything comes back to atoms!

Chemistry and physics combine to impact our biology. On a **TINY** scale! So, by understanding small science, we learn more about how our bodies work and how things can sometimes go wrong.

Small science helps us cure big diseases!

WHAT'S THE **MATTER?**

I DON'T KNOW WHAT **MATTER** IS!

MATTER IS ALL THE STUFF AROUND US AND INSIDE OF US. EVERYTHING THAT YOU CAN SEE AND TOUCH. A BOOK, A PENCIL, THE SUN OR THE EARTH... EVEN YOU. THESE ARE ALL MADE UP OF MATTER! SO, WHEN YOU DRAW WITH A PENCIL, YOU'RE HOLDING MATTER IN YOUR HANDS!

Are these ideas too **big** for you? **Hold on** because we're about to go even smaller...

The scale of things to come

To truly understand small science, we need to shrink to the nanoscale. The nano-what? **The nanoscale!**

Nano literally means 'one billionth of' so when nano is added to the front of a word, it means that something is super-tiny – so small it's impossible to imagine!

How small is the nanoscale? This is a unit of length known as the nanometre. A nanometre is a **billionth of a metre**.

1 metre = 100 centimetres (cm)

1 centimetre = 10 millimetres (mm)

So, there are **1 billion** nanometres in a metre.

Did you know...

○ 1 billion is a thousand million

○ 1 billion seconds is about 32 years!

○ Earth is around 1.3 billion kilometres from Saturn!

1 millimetre = 1,000 micrometres (μm)

THAT'S SMALL, FOLKS!

1 micrometre = 1,000 nanometres (nm)

A billion is **A LOT.** It's...

1,000,000,000!

Teeny things

Black garden ant
(3-5mm)

Pin head
(1-2mm)

Dust mite
(400μm)

Width of human hair
(20-200μm)

Human egg cell
(120μm)

Longest human
chromosome
(10μm)

Red blood cell
(7-8µm)

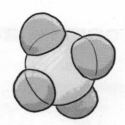

Carbon filament
(5-10µm)

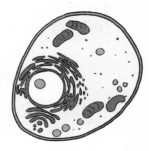

Average human cell
(6µm)

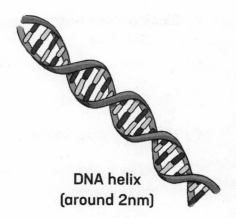

DNA helix
(around 2nm)

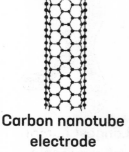

Carbon nanotube
electrode
(1.3nm)

Q: Which of these tiny things
are artificial (made by humans)?

Turn the page
upside down to
see the answers!

35

A: Pin head and
carbon nanotube electrode

Zoom in, zoom out

In 1977, Charles and Ray Eames made a film called
Powers of Ten about the size of different objects
in the universe. They had a passion for science and
technology. The movie started with two people sitting in
a park, having a picnic. Every ten seconds, the camera
zoomed out by a factor of ten.

Eventually, their camera panned back to leave behind...

O **the Earth**

O **the Solar System**

O **the Milky Way Galaxy**

O **...and even the local cluster of galaxies in our part
of the Universe.**

Designer and filmmaker
Charles Eames

In 2010, creator Laura Lynn Gonzalez was inspired by the Eames's work to create **Powers of Minus Ten** - a science app which zooms the other way: down to cells, DNA... and eventually atoms!

See? It all comes back to atoms again!

The tiny size of an atom or a strand of DNA, and the massive scale of our universe, are difficult concepts for our human minds. That's why creative ways to explain them help us to understand our place, and our relative size, in our amazing universe.

Small science, tremendous tech

Our understanding of small science has led to some amazing technological breakthroughs. Scientists are now able to create tiny technology that works at the nanoscale. This technology is called... you guessed it...

nanotechnology!

This is engineering built and maintained between **1 and 100 nanometres** in size. This technology is so small that we need a powerful microscope to see it. It's using atoms to **BUILD** things. A bit like Lego that's invisible to the human eye!

Imagine this, but over a MILLION TIMES more tiny!

SUDDENLY, I DON'T FEEL SO SMALL!

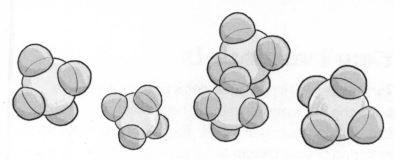

Engineers need to use special equipment to build technology at the nanoscale. Our fingers are far too big, so we would crush anything we built long before we were able to finish it!

This nifty new nanotech has many uses, such as:

○ Infusing socks with nanotech so they keep your feet cool in the summer.

○ Changing the surfaces of tennis balls so they don't wear out as fast.

○ Building car parts with special nanomaterials to make them more fuel-efficient.

But one of the most exciting uses for nanotechnology, both now and in the future, is in medicine. Can you guess what it's called?

That's right! It's...

nanomedicine!

Tiny treatments

Nanomedicine is medicine done at the nanoscale. It has the potential to change how doctors, nurses and scientists do their work. One day, it'll help to diagnose, treat and prevent disease.

Here are some wonderful ways that nanomedicine will change the world:

- **Improving medical scans by showing areas of disease that were too small to be detected before, catching diseases much earlier.**

- **Travelling around the body to find tumours or damage to our blood vessels.**

- **Enhancing bandages to help heal wounds faster.**

- **Building artificial tissues to repair damaged organs.**

And this is where nanotech gets really exciting. Introducing...

NANOBOTS!

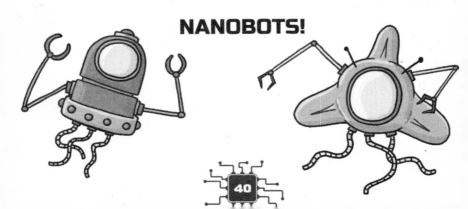

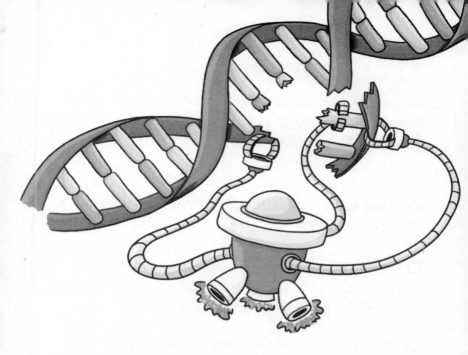

Nanorobotics is the super science of designing and building tiny medical robots. These remarkable robots would be so small you'd need a powerful microscope to see them! Some scientists believe that in the next few decades, our blood will be filled with them. Imagine that! A robot swimming in your bloodstream!

But why?

Well, they could repair our tissues and mend our DNA, so we don't even get sick in the first place. They will exist inside of you, protecting you from damage, ensuring you live a long and healthy life.

They could even track down blocked arteries and remove the blockage before it causes a heart attack or stroke!

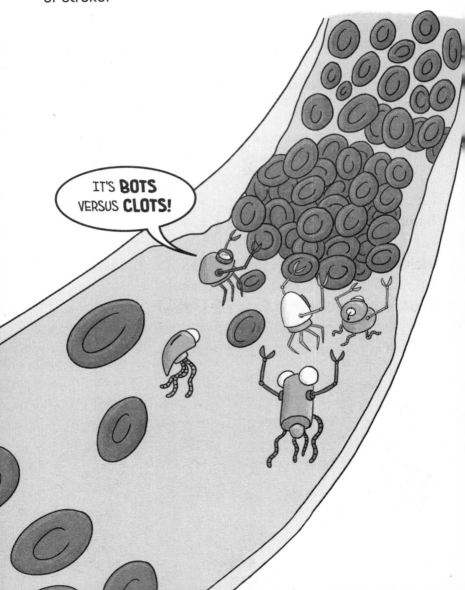

Nanobots could also...

O **Deliver medicines to exactly the right place at the right time.**

O **Monitor vital signs, like blood pressure or heart rate.**

O **Attack and dissolve tumours, helping people with cancer.**

O **Transmit information to our doctors, keeping them informed about our health.**

Once you're filled with nanobots, are you completely human anymore? You'd be part human, part machine.

Wait a minute...

That means you'd be... **A CYBORG!**

Creation station

In science fiction, cyborgs are human-like creatures with technology built into their bodies.

Why don't you **imagine a cyborg of your own** - part human, part machine? What would they look like? **Draw or paint a picture and bring your own cyborg to life!**

And don't forget to give him/her/them a name!

CHAPTER 3

GENE-IUS

We're all totally **UNIQUE!** No one has the same set of fingerprints, your eye colour is specific to you, and even the density of your bones is different to anyone else's. This is all thanks to our **DNA** and **GENES!**

Our genes are fascinating. Not the jeans you wear. The genes inside your cells!

Understanding our **GENETICS** has the potential to make **BIG WAVES** in the field of **MEDICINE**. Perhaps more so than any other medical milestone. It could even be the...

GREATEST MEDICAL DISCOVERY OF ALL TIME!

To understand the gene-ius of our genes, we need to look at some more small science. Let's shrink down into our cells for a moment!

Whoosh!

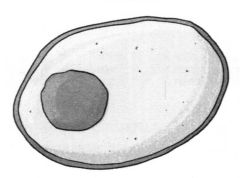

Welcome to a typical human cell. Zoom in further!

Zoom!

You'll find chromosomes inside.

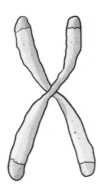

Each human cell contains 46 of them, arranged in 23 pairs. They're super important, as they contain all the information needed to make a human being.

They're made of deoxyribonucleic acid, or DNA for short. DNA is shaped like a twisted ladder, called a double helix.

Each rung on the ladder is made up of chemical units called bases. There are four different types:

A = adenine

T = thymine

C = cytosine

G = guanine

DNA bases exist in pairs. A always pairs with T, and C with G. This is called the base-pairing rule.

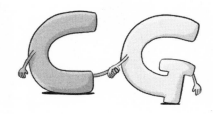

DNA details

Each section of the DNA ladder is called a gene. Genes include information on how you look, such as your eye and skin colour, the shape of your ears, and even how tall you'll ever be. They're a detailed report containing everything about you.

An individual's DNA is completely unique... except in the case of identical twins. Their DNA is - you guessed it - identical! Take the Van Tulleken brothers, famous for their medical show, Operation Ouch. Not only are they identical twins but they're both doctors too. Maybe liking science and medicine was also in their genes!

Q: What do you call twin spies?

A: Double agents!

MY DNA REPORT

Eye colour:	Brown
Ear shape:	Strange
Hair colour:	Black
Height:	Short
Good at science:	Yes
Good at maths:	Hmmm
Good at drawing:	Yes
Likes marmite:	No way!

2+2=22

Blurrgh!!

C- Must try harder!!

Designed by Your DNA

DNA exists in every single cell. It's the blueprint that maps out every organism.

Q: What is an organism?

A: Any living thing such as an animal, plant or YOU!

All the genetic elements that map out an organism are called its genome. This includes bases, DNA, genes... all of it! Every type of organism on Earth has a completely unique genome. For example, an octopus genome is very different to that of a fruit fly. But what about people? Well, the human genome has 3.2 billion bases of DNA, contained in around 20,000 genes.

In fact, understanding the human genome was one of the most marvellous medical milestones ever to occur...

NO FAIR! YOU GOT **TWO** MORE LEGS THAN ME!

BLUEPRINT

The Human Genome Project

This clever collaboration involved scientists from around the world, working together for thirteen years. The project was vital for understanding the exact instructions for making a human being. The main project was completed in 2003, but the entire gene mapping wasn't finished until 2022! The project included:

O Identifying every gene in the human genome.

O Mapping out the sequence of all three billion base pairs - that's a lot of As, Ts, Cs and Gs!

O Developing technology for super-fast genome sequencing.

Genome sequencing

Sequencing is the scientific term for reading someone's genome. It involves working out the order of base pairs In their genome. A machine called a DNA sequencer is used to complete the analysis.

Path of life

You can find the DNA double helix in all sorts of places. For example, in 2005, Cambridgeshire County Council worked with the Wellcome Sanger Institute to build a DNA-inspired cycle path!

The path runs from Addenbrooke's Hospital to Great Shelford four miles to the south. It's painted in colourful stripes that represent the 10,257 bases of a breast cancer gene discovered by scientists at the Institute. If the path had been based on the entire human genome, and not just the breast cancer gene, it would stretch around the Earth **TEN TIMES!**

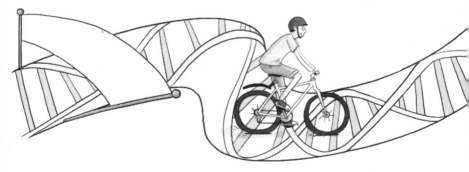

Some diseases like breast cancer happen because a person may have a gene for it. But having the gene doesn't mean everyone will get the disease. There are lots of factors that matter, such as what we eat and where we live. It's important to know all of these details. This is where **PERSONALISED MEDICINE** comes in...

A plan to scan

Personalised medicine lets doctors scan a person to check their insides and see what genes they have. This allows the doctors to tailor the patient's medicine to their unique set of needs. This is called **genomic medicine**. But the genome alone is not enough. To make sense, it's important to combine this data with information about the patient's health.

Genomic medicine

Doctors need both data and technology for personalised medicine to work. They'll use:

O **Genome sequencing** to check a person's genetic make-up.

O **Clinical information** to review signs and symptoms, like a rapid heart rate or a funny tummy.

O **Diagnostics** to find something on a scan, using an MRI (magnetic resonance image) or an ECG (electrocardiogram), for instance.

Now that scientists understand how DNA plays such a huge role in our health, it's possible to:

O Predict how different people will respond to different medicines. This is called pharmacogenomics.

O Help improve the diagnosis of disease.

O Work out who might get certain conditions.

O Tweak treatments until they are as effective as possible.

Keen to intervene

All this incredible information helps doctors and nurses work out what changes - called interventions - are best for the patient. A patient could be asked to:

O Try a new medicine

O Have surgery

O Receive a different treatment

O Make new lifestyle choices

O ...or a combination of all, or some, of these!

Data discoveries

Genomes are tiny but the info they hold is HUGE. So HUGE we need massive hard drives to hold all their data. The study and analysis of these huge datasets is called **bioinformatics.** And did I mention these datasets are HUGE?

Bioinformatics is the science of collecting and analysing complex biological information using computers.

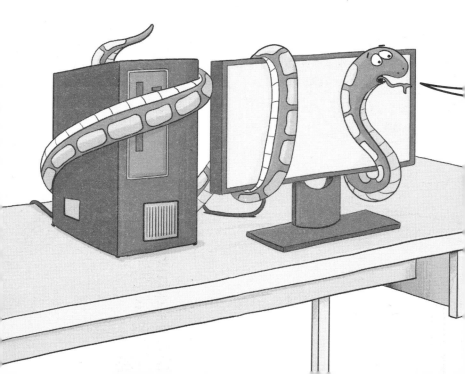

Skills for scientists

Bioinformaticians are scientists who specialise in analysing biological data. One type of programming language they used is called Python, developed by Dutch programmer Guido van Rossum. No, it doesn't involve snakes on your sssscreen. Guido named it after a favourite comedy show: Monty Python's Flying Circus!

Knowledge is power

Data about DNA is the power that fuels personalised medicine. But the science behind **genomics** isn't only being applied to healthcare. This brand-new super science is being used in lots of other incredible ways!

Crime Watch: DNA was first used to catch criminals in 1986. A person can now be identified from a single strand of hair or a tiny flake of their skin. Those baddies had better watch out!

HMM... I THINK **THE BUTLER** DID IT!

Nurturing Nature: Ecologists study streams and analyse water for animal DNA. They can use this data to see where animals are living and monitor the impacts of climate change.

Snot Plot: Marine biologists use drones to fly into the path of a whale's airhole blast to collect its snot! They analyse whale DNA to check their health!

Squeaky Clean: Researchers use the genomic analysis of water to check for microorganisms, ensuring the water is clean enough to drink.

Phase out Farts: By analysing cow genomics, scientists can breed animals that emit less methane, a greenhouse gas. Fewer farts = a healthier planet!

Gene therapies

Gene therapy involves changing the way someone's genes work, perhaps by switching off a faulty gene or turning on a few that should be working but aren't. This is done to improve a person's health.

Gene therapies are being developed to treat diseases, including cancer, by inserting genes that make cancer cells revert back to normal cells. With this technology, the possibilities are endless!

SNIP!

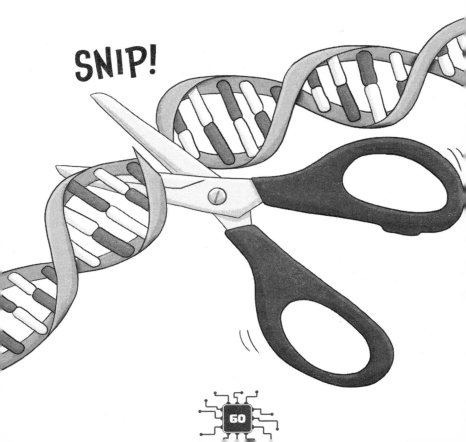

Clever CRISPR

This doesn't involve crisps!
It stands for...

**Clustered Regularly
Interspaced Short
Palindromic Repeats**

Now you understand why it's called CRISPR. Scientists are busy. They don't have time to say the full name every time. They have people to see, places to go, crisps to eat and DNA to copy and paste!

So, what is CRISPR?
It's amazing technology that works
like a pair of molecular scissors. These super scissors
snip apart DNA and insert, delete or modify genes.
Scientists must be careful when they modify a person's
genes. It's important to know which DNA sequences
should be edited and where. Otherwise, anything could
happen! Yes, we all want X-ray vision and the power
of invisibility – but unfortunately this type of genetic
modification is illegal. We've all seen what happens in
the X-Men movies.

The way CRISPR works is simple: you look inside a cell
and find a specific bit of DNA, then you alter it. This
terrific tech has also been adapted to switch genes on
and off, like a super cool light switch. For
example, they can switch off a gene that
causes cancer. This has the potential
to transform how doctors treat and
prevent disease.

Fold for the future

By combining small science with genomics, we'll have even more amazing ways of treating disease.

For example: origami is the Japanese art of paper folding. It's made up of two Japanese words, 'ori' (to fold) and 'kami' (paper). The custom developed over the years, becoming an artform. The principles of origami have now expanded into architecture, engineering and even medicine...

DNA origami involves folding long strands of DNA into different shapes to create nanoparticles. This 'folding' creates a complex structure that can be used to deliver drugs. Imagine it like a puzzle piece. The theory is that if you know the exact size of a piece, you can send it somewhere to slot in perfectly – to deliver a drug molecule to exactly the right place. Fold-tastic!

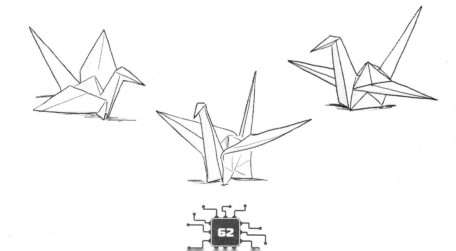

Creation station

Imagine if you had the genes of a pig added to you! Would you have a pig nose and would you suddenly be able to oink? Or perhaps you'll add bee genes and be able to make honey!

Using various photos of animals, make a collage by piecing together different animal body parts. What would your new genetically-modified animal be called?

CHAPTER 4

BIONIC BODIES

BIONICS! These aren't all about robots or mechanical systems, or even superheroes! They can also be about making normal human beings feel even more whole... and fantastic!

Every day now, scientists are replacing body parts and organs with synthetic versions. These **TERRIFIC TECHNOLOGIES** have the potential to **TRANSFORM** people's lives.

Bionics give people the ability to see, hear, touch, move and walk - sometimes for the first time ever.

The future's **BRIGHT**. The future's **BIONIC**.

Bionic body parts appeared in lots of science fiction movies and books. Luke Skywalker had a bionic hand implanted after losing his real one in a lightsaber battle! Now, bionics are no longer science fiction.

But where did the science come from?

It all started with something called **prosthetics**.

Pivotal prosthetics

A prosthetic body part - also known as a prosthesis - is a device that replaces a missing part of the body, such as a lost limb. These were the first attempts at a bionic transformation!

In 2000, a pathologist studying an Egyptian mummy in Cairo discovered it had a toe made of wood and leather! Using carbon dating (a way of measuring how old something is), they worked out that the fake toe was over 3,000 years old!

Wooden toe!

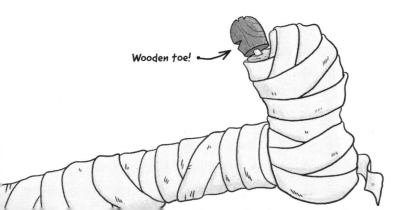

These humans also used early prosthetics:

○ **General Marcus Sergius was a Roman soldier who lost his right hand. So he was given... an iron fist!**

○ **Ambroise Pare made the first hinged prosthetics, back in the sixteenth century. This meant that false limbs could move for the first time!**

Did you know?

○ **Prosthetic is a Greek word and means addition.**

○ **Most prosthetics are needed for amputees – people who have lost one or more limbs.**

○ **Many people think that most amputations happen due to accidents. But in fact three quarters of all amputations are caused by disease such as type 2 diabetes.**

The prosthetics used today are not too dissimilar to those used by the Egyptians, except that the materials used to make them are different (plastic or metal, rather than wood) and the designs have been improved. But there is always room for improvement. And that's where bionics come in. They're super-duper prosthetics!

What's the difference?

Bionic and **prosthetics** can sometimes be confused as being the same, but this is not exactly the case. A bionic device is much more technologically advanced, even though they both mimic the way the organ or limb works.

Bionics allow for more natural movements. In some cases, bionic tech can even be better than the original!

Prosthetics, on the other hand, simply restore the physical aspect of a lost or damaged body part.

Brilliant bionics

A doctor named Jack Steele, from Illinois, USA, came up with the word 'bionics' in 1958! He used it to describe the study of biology that included engineering to solve medical problems. Since then, bionic body parts have been improving all the time.

Here are some examples of brilliant bionics that are currently in development...

- **Bionic eye: a camera sends messages back to an implant in the back of the eye to help someone with vision problems see again.**

- **Bionic ear: this implant stimulates nerves to send sound signals to the brain, allowing someone with hearing problems to hear again.**

- **Bionic limbs (legs and arms).**

- **Artificial organs (heart, pancreas and kidney), to replace damaged organs.**

- **Exoskeleton: a device that helps a person walk.**

- **Neural interfaces: connecting someone's brain to a computer!**

Prosthetic peepers

Scientists have been developing bionic eye technology since the 1980s, but they're yet to create a bionic eyeball that you can stick inside your eye socket, replacing your peepers for good! Current technology involves implants or prosthetics:

BIONIC EYE TECHNOLOGY uses tiny video cameras, often mounted on a person's glasses, to record images. These images are transmitted to little probes on the person's head, right above the part of the brain that receives nerve impulses from the eyes. Incredible!

BIONIC LENSES replace the lenses in the eye for people with cataracts or glaucoma. They can often restore their vision. This technology has the potential to enhance normal vision too. Imagine being able to see over vast distances, or zoom in to see microscopically small things!

Eye-conic!

Bionic eyes will one day replicate the role of the retina, the thin layer of tissue at the back of the eye that receives light and converts it to signals to send to the brilliant brain.

It's likely that a future bionic eyeball will also have super-cool features like access to the metaverse, or augmented reality. It could even transmit your smartphone screen directly into your vision!

Hear, hear! It's a bionic ear

In the 1950s, the cochlear implant was developed for people with hearing loss, the first example of bionic hearing technology. A cochlear implant bypasses damaged parts of the inner ear to activate the auditory nerve. This is the nerve that transfers impulses from our ear to our brain, allowing us to hear.

More recently, bionic hearing has been improved with the invention of auditory brain implants. These devices are allowing some deaf people to hear again by directly stimulating their brains!

Lexi's limb

A British 10-year-old girl called Lexi Pitchford made the news in December 2020 when she received the best Christmas present ever: a brand new bionic arm! Lexi was born without a right hand, as her limb hadn't formed properly in the womb. This meant she found everyday tasks difficult, from brushing her teeth to gripping cutlery.

Lexi had tried prosthetics before, but she found them uncomfortable. Everything changed when she was given a multi-grip bionic limb called the Hero Arm. Life for Lexi is much easier these days!

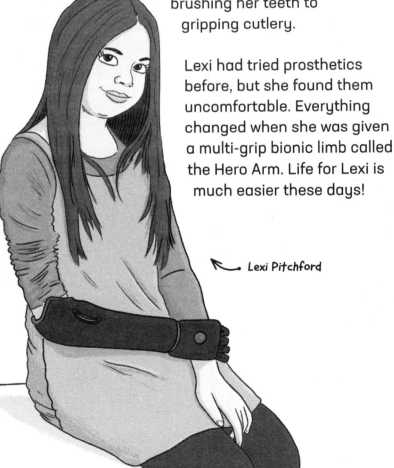

Lexi Pitchford

Put your hand up

Bionic arms like the Hero Arm use sensors to detect muscle movement, allowing the user to control it with ease. This terrific tech can vibrate so that the wearer gets a sense that they are touching an object.

It's hard to replicate a sense of touch... but researchers have created bionic fingertips to allow the wearer to feel different textures. This is still early technology though, as these fabulous fingertips need to be connected to electrodes that are surgically implanted into a person's arm. The sensors in the fingertip generate impulses that move through the hand and arm, mimicking how the nervous system works.

Perhaps one day, the Hero Arm will be fitted with these special fingertips, making the arm and hand even more amazing!

Fun Feels

Collect these items from around your home and use your fingers to feel their surfaces. What do they feel like? Try and describe them!

FEATHER DUSTER   **CUSHION**

ORANGE PEEL

I can HEART-LY believe it

A human heart beats millions of times a year. Sometimes, a person's heart doesn't work properly and needs to be replaced. Heart transplants happen, but people must wait for many months or even years for their replacement heart, as there are not enough spare organs to go around. What would be the answer to this supply problem? A bionic heart, of course...

A bionic heart was difficult to develop — all those moving parts wore out far too quickly. Scientists at the Texas Heart Institute realised that a true bionic heart would need to work differently. They created a prototype that propels blood through the body, rather than pumping it. But what's the difference?

Well, the prototype propels blood in one big **WHOOSH** rather than in slower, more rhythmic **BEATS**, like those of a human heart.

Will this device one day be used to replace damaged hearts? Only time will tell. This tech is so new it hasn't even been tested properly yet!

Programmable pancreas

Diabetes is a condition where a person's blood sugar level isn't controlled properly. People with type 1 diabetes don't create any insulin (the hormone that controls blood sugar levels). Insulin is produced by the pancreas, but in people with diabetes, this awesome organ doesn't work as it should..

But don't worry – technology is coming to the rescue... a potentially life-changing artificial pancreas has now been developed!

This is how it works:

O A sensor is placed under the skin to measure blood sugar levels.

O Data is sent wirelessly to a pump, which works out how much insulin is required.

O The patient can monitor their readings on a smartphone, allowing them to work out how much sugar they should be eating! Sweet!

Mind and body connection

One area of incredible research is how bionic limbs and other body parts can directly connect to our brains. It's important that any bionic technology feels as natural as possible to an amputee or a person with a disability, and gives them the movement they need.

This is where the exciting world of **neural interfaces** comes in - that's literally a connection between a person's mind and a computer.

These amazing devices - known as **neuroprosthetics** - enable people to feel (or see, smell, or taste) the world around them using their bionic technology, as if the tech were part of their own body.

The word 'Neuroprosthetic' means 'nerve addition.' They work by linking directly to a person's nervous system. The computer can stimulate a person's nerves, allowing them to feel sensations.

By using neural activity to move bionic limbs, the experience is more natural and positive for the person using it.

Advances in neural interfaces continue to leap forward, and the technology will soon be used by millions of people around the world!

Marvellous mimics

Biomimicry is when humans use inspiration from nature in their designs and technology, from buildings to clothes, trains to glass, wind turbines to... medical tech! Organisms like insects and crustaceans have a hard outer shell called an exoskeleton, rather than bones deep inside their bodies. By mimicking the biology of these awesome animals, could scientists help humans with mobility issues? Yes!

In 2014, the first bionic exoskeleton was approved. Consisting of motorized leg braces, this nature-inspired invention allows people to walk, stand up and sit down, all using a remote control!

Awesome animal bionics

It's not just humans that have received replacement limbs! Check out these awesome animals:

○ Motola the elephant lost one of her front legs when she stepped on a landmine. After receiving treatment at the Elephant Hospital in Northern Thailand she now has a permanent prosthesis!

○ Touché the tortoise lost one of his legs, so his back end is now attached to a little toy car!

○ Oscar the black cat lost his back legs while sleeping in a field – to a combine harvester! Ouch! Fortunately, Oscar now has two bionic back legs and goes by the name of Prosthetic Puss! (Probably!)

Motola

THAT HARE'S IN FOR A **SHOCK!**

Touché

Oscar

Imagination station

Imagine a superhero with bionic body parts. What would they have and why?

Bionic eye   **Bionic limbs**

Bionic ear   **Neural interface**

Using the outline below, why don't you draw in the various bionics?

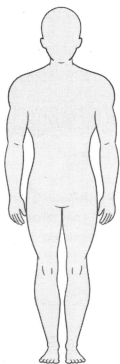

Name .... **Powers** ....

CHAPTER 5

REGENERATE!

Do you ever wish you were just like Doctor Who, with your very own sonic screwdriver, police box and ability to regenerate? Well, now you can be!

OK, so maybe not the first two - but thanks to science we can now **REGENERATE** body bits in a lab!

The Doctor uses regeneration to recreate his or her entire body! We're not quite there (yet!) but in the future there will be ways to replace body parts – from essential organs to missing limbs. This is all thanks to special cells called **STEM CELLS**.

The days of **REGENERATIVE MEDICINE** are only just beginning!

Super stem cells

Stem cells are powerful. That's because these cells have the potential to develop into **ANY** type of cell – such as heart, lung, skin or nerve cells.

That means stem cells can be used to grow **ANY** tissue or organ! Our brilliant bodies need to make new cells to keep working. Stem cells are always waiting and ready to leap to action:

O **They can continuously divide, meaning their supply is endless!**

O **They can change into specialised cells using a process called differentiation, when the body releases chemical signals that instruct them to change into other types of cell.**

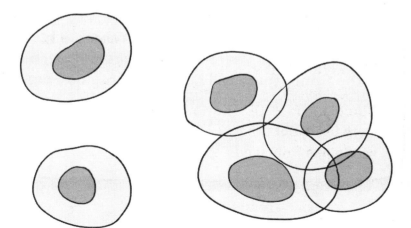

Stem cells are essential for our development, renewal and healing. They enable us to:

O **Build tissue when we're growing in the womb or when we're changing during puberty.**

O **Replace and replenish cells so that they remain strong and fresh.**

O **Heal when we're injured. Think about how new skin forms over a cut or how new bone fuses together if you break a leg!**

Scientists hope that by harnessing the power of stem cells, we can build tissues and organs, and even regenerate body parts!

Terrific trachea transplant

The world's first trachea (windpipe) transplant using a patient's own stem cells was done in Barcelona in 2008. Previously, donor windpipes were used, but the process now involves growing windpipes from a person's own cells!

Let's get organ-ised!

Our organs can be damaged by disease or through accidents. They can even wear out as we get older. For most people, finding a replacement is the only answer. This is called a transplant.

The most common transplanted organs are:

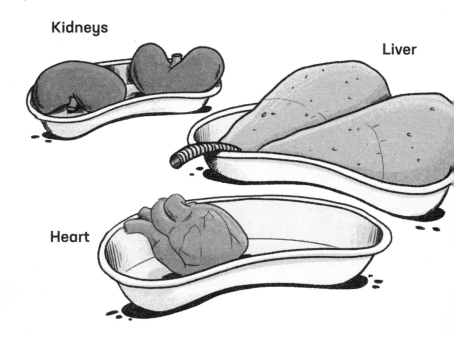

Kidneys

Liver

Heart

Other transplants include the **cornea, intestines, lungs, middle ear, pancreas** and **stomach.**

Did you know?

The lungs are the most difficult organ to transplant as they are most prone to infection after transplantation. Patients can't cough as easily with their new lungs, which means that they can't clear the body of infection.

Organ donation

Millions of people around the world need a transplant to replace a damaged organ.

○ **Organ donation is when a person's organs or tissues are gifted to someone else.**

○ **Organ transplants happen when people are given a new organ to replace a damaged one.**

But unfortunately, there are not enough organs to go around. Many people never get the organ they need.

And in some cases, a person's immune system may reject the organ they're given. That's why it's important to find a genetic match.

Regenerative medicine may have the answer! This type of medicine involves replacing or regenerating human cells, tissues or organs that are damaged or diseased. It could mean that organ donation is assigned to the history books, as organs could be grown to order instead. These lab-grown replacement tissues will be the perfect genetic match for the person who needs them!

Body part anagrams

Mix up the letters to work out several body parts and tissues that have been grown in a lab! One of them hasn't happened yet – can you work out which one?

1. SINK

2. EARTH

3. FRINGE

4. KEEN

5. ARE

6. BELOW

Turn the page upside down to see the answers!

1. Skin, 2. Heart, 3. Finger, 4. Knee, 5. Ear, 6. Bowel. The answer is 3. Finger! Although we may be able to one day grow limbs (arms and legs) and eventually even digits (fingers and toes), we haven't quite done it yet!

Steven's super surgery

Steven Gallagher

Developments in surgery mean body parts can now be transplanted that would have been impossible before. Steven Gallagher had to have both of his hands removed due to a disease called scleroderma. This disease is where the body's own immune system attacks the skin and internal organs. His fingers became so painful that he couldn't use them anymore. But amazingly, Steven was offered a double-hand transplant.

Hands are complex – they have lots of nerves and blood vessels inside them. So linking up two completely new hands with two arms by surgery used to be an impossible feat. This was because the surgery was far too complex. But as doctors and surgeons developed the science, it finally became a reality. Handy!

Fascinating fact!

Xenotransplantation is the scientific word for transplanting tissues or organs from animals into a human.

Did you know?

○ In 1912, the French surgeon Alexis Carrell received the Nobel Prize for his amazing work. Alexis developed a way to connect blood vessels and conducted a successful kidney transplant... in a dog!

○ In 1936, the Ukrainian doctor Yurii Voronoy transplanted the first human kidney.

In the future, hand transplants may not be needed as tissues could be grown from scratch. Imagine if new hands could be completely regenerated? It sounds like something out of a science fiction movie.

But many animals can already regenerate tissues. So scientists are learning all about these remarkable regenerators with the aim of one day mimicking how they do it!

Remarkable regenerators

Did you know...

O Salamanders can grow new tails.

O Octopuses can regenerate their limbs.

O Starfish can sprout completely new limbs.

O Sharks can regrow lost teeth.

TWO CAN PLAY AT THAT GAME!

- Chameleons can grow both their tails and limbs, plus they can change colour too! (So basically, chameleons are superheroes.)

Leg work

Limbs are very difficult to recreate. Why?

- They are made of many different types of tissues – such as bones, muscle and skin.

- They are filled with nerves and blood vessels.

But scientists love a challenge, and in 2022 a group of researchers were able to regrow missing legs in an African clawed frog (Latin name *Xenopus laevis*). The new legs were almost the same length as the originals and allowed the frogs to move and swim normally. This type of research means that one day we should be able to regrow people's limbs too!

Banishing burns

Burns and scalds happen when the skin is damaged due to heat. A burn is caused by dry heat (like an oven) while a scald is caused by something wet (like hot water).

The super skin is made up of three layers:

O **Epidermis**

O **Dermis**

O **Subcutaneous fat layer**

The deeper the layer the burn reaches, the worse the burn. In some cases, burns can be very serious. The skin is never able to fully recover, leaving it scarred.

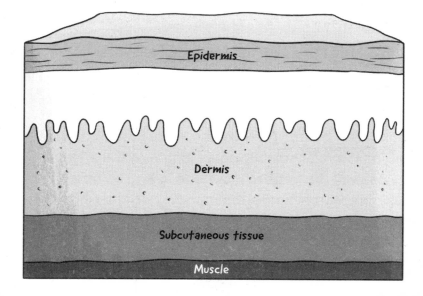

So researchers are looking at how to treat burns using stem cells. Studies have shown that stem cells promote both better and faster healing of burn wounds and they also reduce scarring. There is a lot more research needed, but these amazing cells offer hope to the millions of people with injuries caused by burns and scalds.

Did you know?

O Most people admitted to hospital with burns are young children.

O Almost two thirds of hospital admissions for children with burns or scalds are caused by hot drinks. Be careful with your cuppa!

O Over 90 per cent of burns are preventable, meaning they could have been avoided.

Bioprinting

This amazing technology involves using 3D printers to build and replicate tissue, bone or blood vessels.

How does it work?

1 A computer is given a blueprint of the tissue or organ.

2 The 3D printer reads the digital file and the computer creates a 3D image.

3 Biomaterials are added - these could be layers of cells or collagen.

4 The layers are printed one by one. Each layer sticks to the one below.

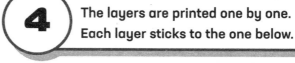

Here are some of the incredible ways that bioprinting is being used in medicine:

- ○ Building extra bone tissue to help people with damaged bones.

- ○ Replacing layers of cells and tissue for people with burns.

- ○ Replenishing blood vessel networks for people whose blood vessels no longer work properly.

Who could imagine we'd be **PRINTING** body parts?

Mini brains!

Brain organoids, also called 'mini-brains,' are little blobs of brain grown in a lab! These brain blobs are helping neuroscientists (brain experts) understand how disease occurs in the brain, hopefully meaning we can learn to stop it!

Creation station

Design a laboratory of the future to grow tissues and organs. What type of equipment will your lab need? Maybe you could include...

O **Microscopes to look at tiny stem cells**

O **Biotanks to grow your tissues and organs**

O **3D printers**

O **Biomaterials to print with - imagine a vat of blood or a roll of skin!**

Draw a map of your lab, including all the amazing machines you'll need!

What does your lab look like?

CHAPTER 6

HOSPITAL OF THE FUTURE

Today's hospitals are filled with patients, looked after by **HEALTHCARE HEROES!** They are doctors, nurses, pharmacists, paramedics, biomedical scientists and other vital workers.

But in the future, hospitals might have robots running the wards, drones delivering drugs or even artificially intelligent doctors diagnosing disease!

It's time to jump forwards through time...
Let's visit the **HOSPITAL** of the **FUTURE!**

Healthcare heroes

Hospitals can't function without all these talented people...

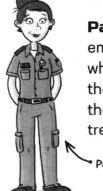

Paramedic

Paramedics give emergency care to people who are injured or ill and then transport them to the hospital for urgent treatment.

Nurse

Nurses care for the sick and injured, in hospital but also outside in the community.

Phlebotomist

Phlebotomists collect blood from patients for tests.

Administrators look after hospital records.

Doctor

Doctors diagnose and treat people who are ill or injured.

Biomedical scientists work in labs. They run tests to support the diagnosis and treatment of disease.

Biomedical

Housekeeper

Porter

Housekeepers
look after the
wards and
manage catering
and cleaning.

Porters
move patients,
equipment
and supplies
around the
hospital.

**Allied health
professionals**
such as physiotherapists
help people to overcome
various medical problems.

Surgeon

Pharmacists
manage,
prepare and
dispense
medicines.

Pharmacist

Surgeons
perform
(sometimes
life-saving)
surgery.

But in the future, not all these jobs will be done by
people! Robots are already in hospitals and artificial
intelligence (AI) is being used to diagnose disease.

But what actually is AI? And what does it mean for
healthcare?

What you're about to see is **TOP SECRET.***

You can't tell anybody about it. Not your mum, dad, aunt, uncle, goldfish or cat. (*Especially* your cat. We all know how cats run a secret society and are always on the verge of taking over the world. This information is **EXACTLY** what they'd need to finally do it.)

Government scientists have been working on a brand-new artificial intelligence that's probably going to replace all doctors in the world. It's called **ARTIDOC** which stands for **ARTIFICIALLY INTELLIGENT DOCTOR...** and we get to try it out!

OK. Ready? Let's switch it on.

Woah. Wrong setting. Always make sure your AI is set to **NICE**. You had it on the **EVIL** setting. *Never* use the evil setting. Let's try again.

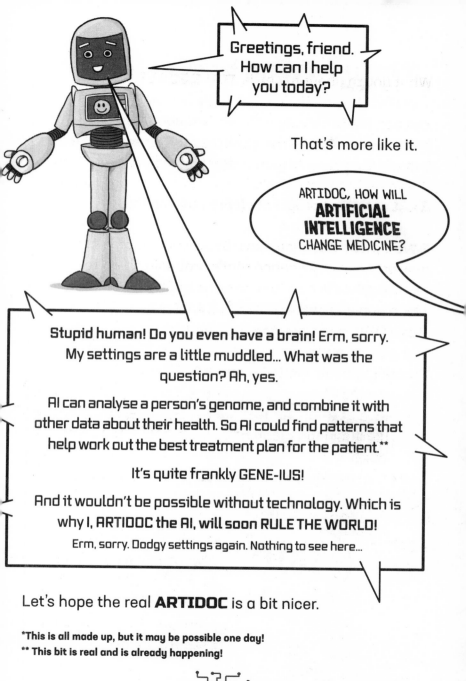

Greetings, friend. How can I help you today?

That's more like it.

ARTIDOC, HOW WILL **ARTIFICIAL INTELLIGENCE** CHANGE MEDICINE?

Stupid human! Do you even have a brain! Erm, sorry. My settings are a little muddled... What was the question? Ah, yes.

AI can analyse a person's genome, and combine it with other data about their health. So AI could find patterns that help work out the best treatment plan for the patient.**

It's quite frankly GENE-IUS!

And it wouldn't be possible without technology. Which is why I, ARTIDOC the AI, will soon RULE THE WORLD!

Erm, sorry. Dodgy settings again. Nothing to see here...

Let's hope the real **ARTIDOC** is a bit nicer.

*This is all made up, but it may be possible one day!
** This bit is real and is already happening!

The boggling brain

Scientists and medical staff are clever. Like, really, really, **REALLY** clever. Clever enough that some of them wanted to find out the answer to the ultimate question: could they replicate their own boggling brains?

Is it possible to recreate **INTELLIGENCE?**

Wait... what **IS** intelligence?

Intelligence is how humans and other animals acquire and apply knowledge and skills. It takes time to learn and do things. Like riding a bike without falling off, or getting better at painting a picture. We need our intelligence to **THINK** about **WHAT** we're going to do and **HOW** we're going to do it. That means we can improve at whatever task we set our minds to. Humans can do it. So can many animals.

But the next question scientists came up with was...

Can Machines Think?

In 1950, Alan Turing PhD OBE, known as 'the father of computer science', published his most famous work: Computing Machinery and Intelligence. In his paper, he asked a very important question: can machines think for themselves?

Alan was an English mathematician and cryptanalyst (codebreaker) who lived from 1912 to 1954. He became a scientist and is famous for cracking the Enigma code in World War II. But that's not all. He also created the 'Turing Test'. This was a way to check if machines could think.

Could they?

Turing wasn't sure. His theory was that a computer can mimic human behaviour, but not think for itself.

Artificial intelligence

In 1955, the scientist John McCarthy first coined the phrase 'Artificial Intelligence'. Then AI developed rapidly over the years!

O In 1997, a system called Deep Blue beat the world's best chess player. Take that, human brain!

O In 2011, with the invention of Siri, voice-assisted AI entered people's homes!

But for now, computers just can't do all the things we can. For example, how do you recognise a family member or friend? Maybe it's...

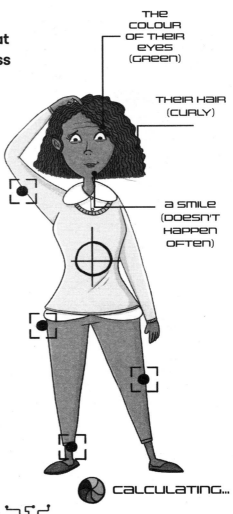

THE COLOUR OF THEIR EYES (GREEN)

THEIR HAIR (CURLY)

a SMILE (DOESN'T HAPPEN OFTEN)

CALCULATING...

These are all things a computer could be taught to recognise. But, probably, you can spot other, smaller details too... for example, if someone owes you birthday money!

Scratching hair (means they're nervous)

A pained grin (didn't want to open their wallet)

Sadness in the eyes (about to lose money!)

All of these extra details come from human processing. Could an AI really see all the signs that birthday money is about to arrive?

Can a computer notice all the differences humans can?

Not yet, but **SOON**.

Technology is advancing every day. Maybe it won't be long before AIs can **THINK!**

Future doctors?

Human doctors take years to learn how to be a doctor. But imagine an AI who could access all the knowledge in the world in an instant. They could learn how to be a doctor in a millionth of a second.

That's faster than Doctor Who travels in their **TARDIS!**

But **WHY** would we want robot doctors?

Ever heard of a 'bedside manner'? This is the way that contact with another human being – a kind, expert and reassuring doctor or nurse – can help someone start to feel better. But sometimes treating illness or disease needs to be done quickly and accurately – faster than humans can work. That's where AI can come in!

Computers vs covid

In the early days of COVID-19, no one yet knew how this disease travelled or worked. So hospitals in New York built AI systems. One of them analysed the sound of people's coughs to see if they had COVID-19. Another one studied scans of patients' lungs. Out of 25 patients who had been given the all-clear, the AI system discovered that 17 of them had COVID-19!

Documents and Data

In the olden days, doctors and nurses would write notes about their patients on paper, to be added to big bulky folders full of patient records. But not anymore.

With the invention of electronic patient records, everything about a patient is now held on a computer. If it isn't all there yet, it will be soon. Why is this important?

DATA, that's why.

But what is data? It's any type of information.

The more data you have, the easier it is to make informed decisions, like what treatment is needed after seeing a scan or which drug will probably work best for a disease.

Data is knowledge. And **KNOWLEDGE** is **POWER!**

AI innovations

AIs are currently **mining data** to help doctors diagnose and treat disease! But what is data mining?

Well, miners dig for coal (sometimes finding dinosaur bones instead!)

But today, scientists mine **DATA** to find patterns!

Divine Data

In 2022, scientists at the Institute of Cancer Research in London created an AI that uses large amounts of data (called datasets) to predict which drugs are most likely to work for cancer patients.

The information included details about different types of tumours (abnormal growths in the body). Once the AI got to work, it was able to predict how a patient might respond to a medicine based on their tumour type!

Successful Scans

Every year, millions of people are diagnosed with breast cancer (mostly women, but some men too). Tissue samples are taken from the tumour and studied, so that the right treatment can be given.
Now, scientists at the Karolinska Institute in Sweden have developed AI-based technology that analyses scans of tumours more accurately. The AI compares the scan against a collection of other tumour images. It then puts patients into high and low risk groups, allowing doctors to focus on patients who are most at risk first. This will help save lives!

AIs will change the future of medicine. We can only imagine...

The following story is **SCIENCE FICTION** but may one day be **SCIENCE FACT!**

Emergency

It's 2075 and a girl is climbing a tree...
WHOOPS! She falls and breaks her arm!
A medical drone spots the girl and calls 999!

Ambulance

Robot paramedics arrive at the scene and check the patient. Once they know it's safe to do so, they move her to a self-driving ambulance, where she's placed on a hoverbed.

Diagnosis

The ambulance scans the girl and works out where her injuries are. The ambulance transmits medical information to the hospital, so staff there are ready for her arrival. Data floods into the hospital computer, alerting the AI doctor. The ambulance zips along the road to the hospital.

Hospital

The girl's hoverbed flies through the hospital doors. The AI doctor has already worked out that the girl's bone is badly broken and needs surgery. Robot porters move her to the operating theatre.

Operate

A robotic surgeon performs surgery and within a few hours, the girl's arm is in a cast! Robot nurses look after the girl until she's ready to be discharged.

Recovery!

Back at home, a robot physiotherapist helps the girl to move her arm again. She has some pain, so a drone delivers painkillers directly to her! Incredible!

Imagination station

Your teacher has given you so much homework to do you're not sure you'll be able to do it all!
If you could have an AI help you with your homework, what would you ask it to do and why?

O **Do your algebra for maths class?**

O **Write a short story for your English lesson next week?**

O **Paint a picture for your art teacher?**

Draw what an AI doing your homework would look like!

CHAPTER 7

ROBOTS & GADGETS

Robots build our cars, deliver food and even travel to other planets to run science experiments! Soon, they will be living in our homes and caring for us when we're sick.

These **REMARKABLE ROBOTS** come in all shapes and sizes. From robot companions befriending care home residents, to drones delivering drugs.

And it's not just robots... other terrific technologies will change how doctors prevent, diagnose and treat disease. There are already a host of **GREAT GADGETS** used in healthcare. And these devices only get better with time!

What is a robot, anyway?

A robot is a machine that can carry out jobs on its own.

O **Robots can be given instructions to do specific tasks.**

O **They are usually guided by a computer - either one built inside it (for example, in a robotic lawn mower) or one located somewhere else (such as when NASA controls a robot on Mars).**

One day, your teacher might be a robot. Or maybe they already are...

Anyone without their homework will be terminated. You have 20 seconds to comply!

Did you know?

O The word 'robot' comes from the Slavic word 'robota' meaning 'to work'.

O The first robots were called automatons and were driven by clockwork, air or water.

O Around 400 BC, Greek inventor Archytas of Tarentum built a steam-powered wooden pigeon that could fly!

O Around 1206 AD, Islamic inventor Ismail Al-Jazari created clocks powered by water. They had mechanical figures and little whistling birds that sang on the hour!

O A robot that looks like a human is called an android.

Q: Why did the robot fail his exam?

A: Because he was a little rusty.

Famous made-up robots

One of the most famous robot characters is the Tin Man from The Wizard of Oz. But he was originally a man who later gets a heart... so does that mean he was actually more of a cyborg?

TURN TO PAGE 65 FOR MORE **BRILLIANT BIONICS!**

I, Robot

The author Isaac Asimov often had robot characters in his stories. In the short story Runaround (1942), Asimov wrote three laws that robots would need to follow if they were going to live in harmony with humans!

The Three Laws of Robotics

1. A robot may not injure a human being or, through inaction, allow a human being to come to harm.

2. A robot must obey the orders given it by human beings except where such orders would conflict with the First Law.

3. A robot must protect its own existence as long as such protection does not conflict with the First or Second Law.

Even though these laws were written in a science fiction story, they make sense!

Now that we're living in a real age of robots, we should probably put similar laws into practice!

What's up, doc?

How different would it be to be treated by a robot doctor? Will it feel the same? Does it matter? These are the questions scientists need to ask as they develop artificial intelligence and robots that may one day support real doctors in healthcare...

But did you know that there are **ALREADY** robots working in hospitals?

Robot Pharmacist

A robot at Guy's Hospital in London helps patients get their medicines faster! This state-of-the-art pharmacist has a long arm that moves around the pharmacy's drug store, collecting medicines from the shelves to dispense to a human pharmacist for checking.

The Da Vinci Code

A robot with arms called da Vinci is used in some hospitals to perform more precise operations. Although the device is robotic, it is always controlled by a human surgeon. But as technology advances, maybe one day da Vinci or its descendants will do everything by itself!

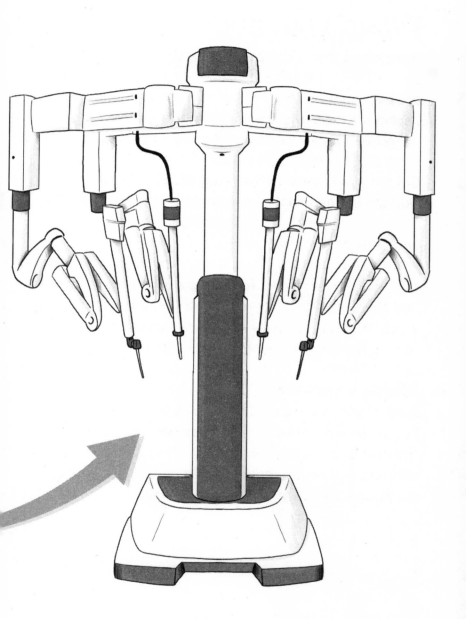

And robots help with social care out in the community too!

Meet Stevie

Developed by Trinity College Dublin in Ireland, Stevie is a white robot that rolls around on wheels. He has movable arms and a screen on his head with a cartoon face!

In 2018, Stevie spent time with care home residents to understand how machines could one day help older people to deal with loneliness.

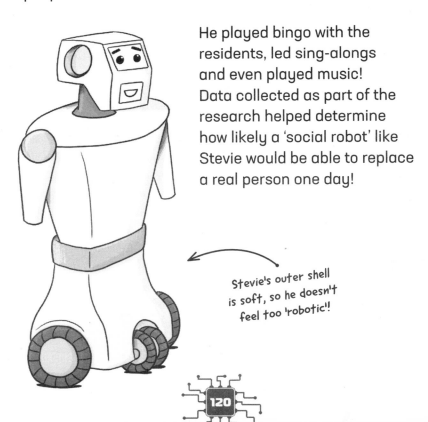

He played bingo with the residents, led sing-alongs and even played music! Data collected as part of the research helped determine how likely a 'social robot' like Stevie would be able to replace a real person one day!

Stevie's outer shell is soft, so he doesn't feel too 'robotic'!

Health and social care

Healthcare and social care are both important for people's health and wellbeing. Healthcare usually covers doctors' surgeries and hospitals, while social care includes all the support people need to cope with illness, disability, old age or poverty.

Drones Delivering Drugs

In 2022, the NHS in England tested out a drone that could be used to provide life-saving medicine in super-quick time. The drone delivered chemotherapy drugs (to treat cancer) from Portsmouth all the way to the Isle of Wight.

Usually the delivery takes four hours, with two car journeys and a ferry across the sea. But the drone managed to cut the travel time down to 30 minutes! Amazing!

Q: Why do robots make bad teachers?

A: They DRONE on and on...

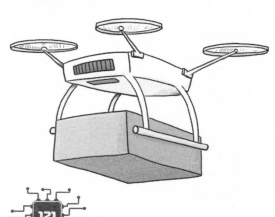

Remarkable robot research

Scientists continue to research all the different ways that robots can help us and our world. Here are just three different robots that exist NOW and could help build our FUTURE...

Rovables to the Rescue

Robots can reach places that humans cannot, like the surface of Mars or the bottom of the ocean. Soon they could be roaming around inside your body too! Introducing **rovables**: small robots that can move about on their own. Much larger than nanobots, these robots are still small enough to move around inside the body. In the future, we could swallow rovables that move around our digestive tract, fixing holes in our stomach or repairing damaged tissues. We may never need normal surgery again!

Cool Crabs

Researchers at Northwestern University in Illinois, USA, have created tiny crab-like robots that may one day clear clogged arteries or find and destroy cancerous tumours! If the idea of tiny robot crabs climbing about inside your body is too much, don't worry. It's still a long time before they will actually get inside a real human!

Sweaty Robots

Scientists at the University of Tokyo in Japan created a 'sweaty' robot finger! In the future, robots will take on some of the tasks of doctors, nurses and other health professionals. In order to help patients trust them, it would be great if these robots could look and feel like a human being. The finger has a layer of skin over it that sweats like a real human finger does. This incredible research blurs the line between flesh and machine. It's another small step towards a real-life cyborg!

Technology test!

1. An android is a robot that looks like a...

   a.   Human

   b.   Gorilla

   c.   Puppy

   d.   Tyrannosaurus Rex

2. Where **WON'T** you see a robot working?

   a.   In a factory

   b.   In a hospital

   c.   Under your bed

   d.   At a restaurant

3. How do you give robots instructions?

   a.   Use a carrier pigeon

   b.   Shout very loudly

   c.   Talk to it in a robot voice

   d.   With a computer program

4. Which famous Renaissance artist (and Ninja Turtle) is a surgeon robot named after?

   a. Raphael
   b. Donatello
   c. Michelangelo
   d. Leonardo da Vinci

COWABUNGA, DUDE!

5. What kind of tasks can robots **NOT** do yet?

   a. Perform surgery
   b. Go to school instead of you
   c. Chat to people in care homes
   d. Deliver drugs

Turn the page upside down to see the answers!

Answers box: 1a, 2c, 3d, 4d, 5b

Help to be healthy

Life in the future will involve lots of exciting technology. One tech type that's booming is the healthcare gadget.

By monitoring different aspects of a person's health, these gadgets can help us stay healthier for longer. This is because they keep track of important readings and alert people if there are problems.

The most popular gadgets now are used to monitor:

- O Heart rate
- O Blood sugar
- O Blood pressure
- O Body temperature

DNA Devices

As personalised medicine becomes more important, doctors will need a quick way to check someone's genome. Portable DNA devices are now in development, meaning that a person's DNA can be analysed in record time in a GP practice or surgery. Using a mobile app, the decoder can be used to detect genetic diseases.

Wonderful wearables

Wearable technology is any electronic device that a person can wear, like a smartwatch, that collects data about a person's health and exercise.

These devices are often linked to an app on a mobile phone. They can even send health information to a doctor or nurse for them to review.

In the future, wearable technology could sit on the surface of your skin, or even on your fingernail.

Many apps are already used to monitor health, from step monitors to sleep checkers.

Creation station

Design a medical robot!

O If you could build a medical robot, what would it look like?

O Would it have metal legs or caterpillar tracks, or would it fly like a drone?

O Using pipe cleaners, paper, cardboard and sticky tape (or any other materials you have to hand), build your own medical robot. Don't forget to give it a name! Maybe you could even make it a uniform!

CHAPTER 8

MEDICINE
IN THE
METAVERSE

The **METAVERSE** is like the internet, but in 3D.
It's a virtual space created by computers. People
use immersive technology like virtual reality
(VR) to get inside.

There's one part of the metaverse that
may one day save lives... the
MEDICAL METAVERSE.

What will it be like in this **VIRTUAL WORLD?**
And how will it help us live longer, happier lives?
Time to **PLUG IN** and find out!

Before we dive into this virtual world, let's look at some of the different words that will pop up from time to time.

VIRTUAL REALITY is where you are completely immersed in a virtual environment.

AUGMENTED REALITY is where the visible natural world is overlaid with digital content, such as in mobile phone games where you collect tokens by exploring the physical world around you!

Virtually healthy!

So how could you use VR in healthcare?

Fitness and physical health: people will be able to exercise inside the metaverse. For example, someone stuck at home could still exercise in a virtual gym!

Mental health: Researchers are looking at VR as an alternative treatment for attention deficit hyperactivity disorder (ADHD), a condition where people struggle to focus. The VR simulates a classroom and teacher while various distractions appear, like a buzzing bee or a noisy sound system. The goal of the VR is to 'train' children to learn to ignore these distractions and focus on the teacher instead. Clever!

Support and wellbeing: hospital stays can be unpleasant for some people, but VR and gaming could make their time in hospital more fun!

Very Remarkable (VR) Facts!

O 'Augment' means 'to make better, larger or more intense'.

O The Telesphere Mask, the first VR headset, was invented by American filmmaker and inventor Morton Heilig in the 1960s.

O In 1995, a company called Virtual I/O created the first pair of VR glasses called iGlasses.

Terrific telemedicine

Telemedicine involves doctors and other healthcare professionals reviewing and treating patients virtually, using computers or smartphones. It uses lots of terrific technology including video calls, the internet and live streaming to monitor patients.

Some health checks can be done remotely if they don't require checking a patient in person. These visits are even being done using VR!

Telemedicine means patients no longer need to be in a specific location, so doctors can treat patients wherever they are - even in another country!
All they need to do is put on a VR headset!

Digital twins

Have you ever met your doppelganger - someone who looks exactly like you?

No?

Well, they might be out there somewhere... but imagine if you could create an exact copy of yourself on a computer. A digital twin!

But why?

To help manage your health, of course. We now live in an age where anything and everything can be copied to the metaverse. Including YOU!

A digital twin is a copy of something, or someone, from the real world in a virtual world. The reason they are created is to provide information. In the case of the metaverse, a digital twin could be used to see how someone will recover from surgery or even how they may react to certain medicines. As we feed genetic information into the medical metaverse, the computer will learn how to treat patients better.

By observing what happens to a digital twin first, real-life patients could recover faster and live longer.

Don't skip a beat

In 2014, scientists created a virtual model of a human heart for surgeons to practice heart surgery before they tried it for real! Dr Steve Levine was inspired to create this terrific tech after his daughter was born with congenital heart disease. He created digital hearts using VR to help surgeons work out exactly where they needed to perform lifesaving surgery.

This terrific tech is being used across the world, including at Boston Children's Hospital in the US, and Great Ormond Street Hospital in London!

Digital twins of twins!

In 2022, three-year-old twins Bernardo and Arthur Lima had surgery to separate them, after they were born joined at the head. The surgery was done at a hospital in Rio de Janeiro, Brazil, with help of surgeons over 9,000 km away at Great Ormond Street Hospital, London.

How did they do this?

Using VR, of course!

Surgeons at Great Ormond Street were familiar with this type of procedure, so they advised the doctors in Brazil, step by step. In total, the twins needed a number of surgeries, taking over 27 hours of operating time. Both teams spent many months working together and practising using the VR system. They even used VR projections of the twins...

Perhaps this is the first example of digital twins of twins!

IN SOME WAYS THESE OPERATIONS ARE CONSIDERED THE **HARDEST** OF OUR TIME, AND TO DO IT IN **VIRTUAL REALITY** WAS JUST REALLY MAN-ON-MARS STUFF.

Surgeon
Noor ul Owase Jeelani

Level up!

The word **gamification** means to turn something into a game. We all do this, all the time:

○ **On a long car journey, you can play at spotting the most red cars that pass.**

○ **You could race to complete a task, if you and a friend are doing the same thing.**

○ **Mary Poppins used the song 'A Spoonful of Sugar' to turn tidying a room into a game.**

See? Gamification!

DON'T STOP UNTIL YOU'VE REACHED 10,000 STEPS!

And technology can help with this...

The gamification of healthcare is about improving or maintaining health through competitions, games and rewards. This can be done on a computer or using apps on a smartphone.

For example, if a doctor tells a patient they should walk more, they could download an app that tracks their steps, gaining rewards or points as they increase their step count over time.

These little positive nudges in the right direction will help people stay motivated while also changing their behaviour, like doing more exercise or eating more greens!

The virtual hospital

The hospital of the future may not be completely physical. Some of it may only exist in the metaverse!

In emergencies, patients usually need to be rushed to hospital. But for patients who have less urgent health issues, they could see doctors or nurses in the metaverse first, before making a journey to the hospital.

Some treatments could even be delivered virtually, like counselling and physiotherapy. For example, physiotherapists could observe patients at their homes using cameras, to see if they can move after an injury.

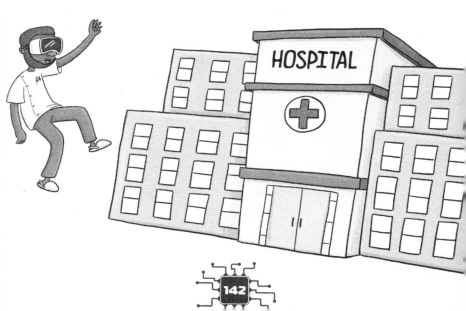

Earth 2.0

It's not only people that are getting digital twins inside the metaverse. One of the most ambitious projects to date involves building a complete digital version of our ENTIRE PLANET!

A company in the United States has created the Omniverse, a place of virtual locations and digital twins. They plan to photograph the entire surface of the Earth using high resolution satellites, to replicate the planet inside the metaverse...

Picture perfect!

Creation station

Why not design your own virtual reality system? It could feature amazing graphics, a cool headset, a superfast computer, and maybe even a full-body suit so you could feel what it's like to be in VR!

Once you've designed your VR system, what would you use it for? If you could go anywhere in the metaverse - any kind of made-up place, game world or virtual version of the real world - where would you go and why?

CHAPTER 9

NURTURED BY NATURE

To be healthy, humans must eat well, do regular exercise and have plenty of sleep. But that's not everything. We also need satisfying surroundings if we truly want to thrive.

Our **ENVIRONMENT** affects **OUR HEALTH**. How we live and where we live. This means we need to protect the world around us, so the world can protect us too.

This is **NATURE MEDICINE!**

The environment is everything

Planet Earth is under threat from problems like pollution and climate change.

This may feel scary. And when scary things happen, the world can sometimes feel overwhelming.

But don't despair! Scientists can come to the rescue! **(AGAIN!)**

The more we understand issues like climate change, the more we can do to improve our environment. And there is SO MUCH to be excited about! Yes, there are issues... but there are solutions too. Time for some **CLIMATE OPTIMISM!**

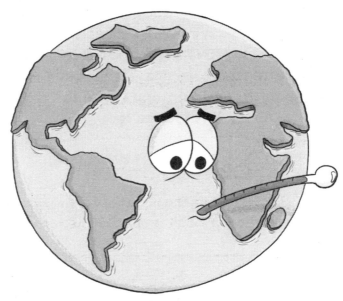

Climate calamities and super solutions!

All these climate calamities have super solutions.
We just need to make them happen! Can you work out
which one goes with which?

Climate calamity

1. Climate change

2. Loss of biodiversity

3. Destruction of forests

4. Overfishing

5. Pollution

Super solution

a. Stop cutting down trees

b. Cleaner machines

c. Protect nature reserves

d. End use of fossil fuels

e. Allow fish stocks to replenish

Turn the page upside down to see the answers!

Did you know?

Biodiversity is the variety of life in a
particular habitat or ecosystem.

Answers: 1d, 2c, 3a, 4e, 5b

Future farms

As world temperatures soar, crops may be affected, meaning there's less food. Scientists are now able to engineer crops that are more drought resistant using gene editing. This means that they change a crop's DNA. Genetically Modified Organisms (GMOs) are seeds, plants, animals or microorganisms that have been created by gene editing or inserting completely different genes from other organisms. These tweaks allow the organism to exhibit new traits which can:

O Improve the taste of vegetables

O Boost levels of vitamins and minerals

O Allow crops to survive under warmer conditions

O Increase crops' resistance to disease and pests

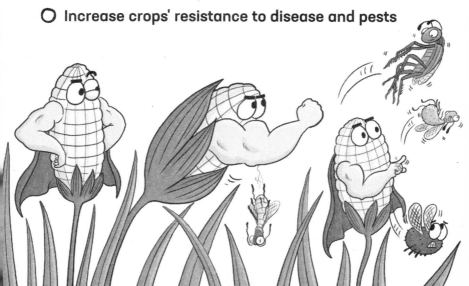

Harmful heat

Rising temperatures can make a difference to health. In 2019, Professor François Roubille and a team of researchers at Montpellier University Hospital in France studied the impact of super warm temperatures on people who had heart failure (that's when the heart can't pump blood around the body well, so people need medicines to help).

They found that changes in temperature affected heart failure patients more than most others.

Extreme temperatures make everyone more dehydrated, and heart failure patients are at particular risk. So the researchers asked patients to input their weight into a computer during the hottest times.

By tracking patients' weight, doctors were able to work out when they were losing too much water and getting dehydrated. Then they could respond quickly to any health issues. Another example of how technology is helping doctors treat patients faster!

Finish those farts

Did you know that **FARTS** are causing climate change? (No, not your brother's. Even though they're pretty bad.)

It's **COW FARTS** we need to worry about. OK, not just cows. All types of livestock: cattle, sheep, pigs and goats.

These gross gasses, otherwise known as methane emissions, are produced in the stomachs of livestock when they break down plants. The animals burp out most of the gas, but the rest emerges as terrible toots. That means to reduce climate change, we need to reduce the number of livestock we keep.

But what does that mean for food?

BURRP!

PARP!

Gross gasses

Gross gasses aren't the only problem. Humans need to produce food for all this livestock, too. So, when droughts affect crops, it has a knock-on effect. Our animals can't eat!

With climate change, our food sources will need to change. We need to think about what we eat, to make sure that all food is sustainable.

We may not be able to predict the exact future, but one thing is for certain, our diets will change as a result...

TRUMMP!

POOT!

The future of food

What's on the menu of tomorrow's restaurants?

Today, many people are choosing a healthier, more sustainable diet that includes less meat. Could you replace your quarter pounder with a plant burger?

O **Quinoa Burgers: these are gluten-free, high in protein, have a nice texture and are easy to cook.**

O **Lentil Patties: lentils are one of the most nutrient-dense foods on the planet. They're full of vitamins, minerals, fibre, protein and iron. And they're tasty!**

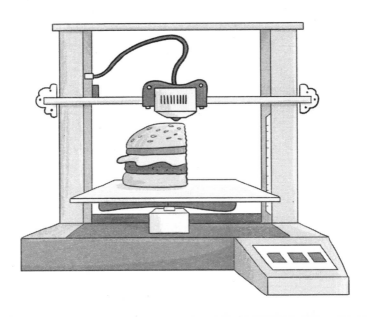

Print your patty

In the future, we may have 3D printed vegan steaks instead of real meat. Redefine Meat, an Israeli company, has created the 'Alt-Steak' which is 'printed' with soy and pea protein. This fake steak looks, feels and tastes like meat. But it's way more environmentally friendly to produce and because it's plant-based, it's healthier for humans too!

Bugs in your belly!

Instead of pulling out a bag of crisps for a snack, future school kids might get out a bag of bugs instead!

But why would we want to eat bugs? Well, bugs emit less harmful gas than livestock. For example, a cow produces 2.8 kg of gross gas per kilo, while a kilo of bugs only produce 2 grams.

Beetles: roasted or dried, they're full of protein, vitamins and minerals.

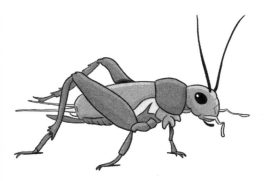

Crickets: a good source of protein, iron and vitamin B12, these brilliant bugs are great when ground down into flour. They're so good that crickets may soon make up most breads, cakes and pastries!

Grasshoppers: a delicacy in Mexico, South America and some parts of Africa, grasshoppers are excellent when fried in oil with garlic, lemon and salt.

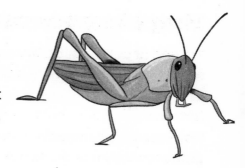

Mealworms: these wiggly larvae are full of omega-3 fatty acids, protein and minerals like copper, sodium and potassium. They make the perfect crunchy crisps or even a tasty spread when ground into a powder and mixed with chocolate!

Termites: it's usually the termites that munch through things, but soon we may be munching them instead. High in protein, they can be served smoked or sun-dried.

Helping to heal with nature

Trees and woodlands and rivers and waterfalls and starry skies. The natural world is beautiful and it brings us a sense of calm and ease.

This has been known for millennia, but today, instead of some medications, doctors are now prescribing **NATURE** to help us heal. Nature medicine is a brand-new field involving the use of natural settings. Research shows that walking in natural settings like a forest reduces stress and improves heart health. Even exercising near water or woodlands is more effective than exercising indoors. Here are some real examples of nature therapies!

O **Meditation in natural settings to reduce stress and anxiety**

O **Woodland walks with friends to help alleviate depression**

O **Swimming in a lake to improve physical fitness**

The world around us has even been shown to improve our performance: enhancing memory, increasing focus, improving motivation and even boosting creativity. So if you're painting a picture by a lake, it might just be a masterpiece!

Natural adventures

But nature therapy doesn't just mean going outside! There are many different examples of how we can use nature to help us feel better, including:

- O Adventure therapy: improving physical fitness and mental wellbeing

- O Animal-assisted or pet therapy: using animals or pets to heal

- O Therapeutic horticulture: gardening to improve physical and mental health

Protected by pets

Research shows that interacting with animals improves people's mental health. But animal therapy goes even further. It involves using animals or pets to help people cope with and recover from both physical and mental health conditions.

Here are some amazing animals who help heal humans!

- **Cats** act as good companions for people with dementia.

- **Dogs** help people with anxiety, depression and autism.

- **Horses** have been taken to cancer clinics to help patients undergoing chemotherapy.

Cheers for Chester

A therapy dog named Chester helped a little boy called Alex who had autism. Before Chester came along, Alex's autism meant he experienced high levels of anxiety and he became non-verbal (he stopped speaking).

In 2017, Chester moved in with Alex and his family. He was a dog who was professionally trained to help Alex manage his stress and anxiety. Not only did Chester help Alex feel safe, but their relationship also helped Alex learn to speak again!

Working with the world

What next? One guess is that we will learn more about how to collaborate with nature. Once we can master new ways of living in harmony with the world around us, everyone's lives will improve.

We have the science, technology and information to protect our planet. We just need to take action. The science is clear. Save nature, save our health. Save our health, save humanity!

Imagination station

It's time to try out your own nature therapy! You'll need a sheet of paper and some coloured crayons.

Why don't you go on a walk with your family into a green space - either a park or woodlands - and really soak up nature?

Go and hug a tree - that's right, hug it! Imagine you're connected. Close your eyes and feel its energy. Breathe it all in!

Now take a bark rubbing using your paper and crayons. Beautiful!

CHAPTER 10

FOREVER FRIENDS

If curing all diseases wasn't enough, scientists want to go one step further and...
END AGEING!

One day, we may extend our lifespans using future medicines. Or perhaps we'll upload a digital copy of ourselves to the Metaverse - living for eternity inside cyberspace.

Imagine a world where you and your friends are **IMMORTAL** - never ageing, never dying. Science could make this dream a reality, but would you even want to **LIVE FOREVER?**

What is ageing?

It's the process where organisms become older, changing with the passage of time.

Biological aging is caused by damage to our cells. They can no longer repair themselves, resulting in ageing.

Did you know?

Age can be measured in two ways: chronological age (the passage of time) or biological age (how healthy we are as we age). They can be different!

A 'young' person may have an older biological age if they don't exercise, while an 'older' person may have a younger biological age if they eat well and keep fit.

Fantastic Facts!

○ The study of human ageing is called gerontology.

○ Lifespans vary hugely across the natural world. Adult mayflies live for about 24 hours, while some corals can survive for over 4,000 years! Some animals, as we'll see shortly, can even be immortal...

○ The world's human population is getting older and older. Why? Because of improvements in medicine. An illness that might have meant the end of someone's life can now be cured.

○ Research shows that being positive about getting old actually makes you live longer!

Myths, legends and science

Humans have been fascinated with immortality (living forever) from the beginning of time. The idea of immortality has been part of many different cultures for thousands of years.

One Greek legend told the story of how Achilles was granted limited immortality after his mother Thetis dipped him in the Styx River (a mythical place where Earth crossed over into the Underworld). While this was just a story, modern-day science may be close to making the dream of eternal life possible. If only the ancient Greeks could see us now!

But the million-dollar question is...

Can we cheat death?

The geriatric jigsaw

Longevity is the scientific word for how long an organism lives.

Genes linked to longevity have been discovered in some organisms. For example, biologists studying fruit flies found genes that control how long they live. By making tiny changes to their genes, the scientists were able to double their lifespan!

Genes alone are only part of the puzzle. Many factors affect how we age, such as how much sleep we get, what we eat and how much exercise we do. Scientists are only starting to learn how all these puzzle pieces fit together...

Did you know?

O **Paediatrics** is the study of the health of babies and children.

O **Geriatrics** is the study of elderly people's health and wellbeing.

Excellent epigenetics

Epigenetics is the science of how the way we live affects how our genes work.

Although we can't usually change our genes, our lifestyles can affect them.

For example, someone may have a gene that causes cancer. It may cause cancer in some people and not others, sometimes depending on how they live - for example, if they smoke or not.

That means some of our choices in life may affect how our genes play out!

Telomere trophy

In 2009, Professor Elizabeth Blackburn was awarded the Nobel Prize in Physiology or Medicine. Elizabeth was born in 1948 in Tasmania, Australia. She has worked all around the world and received a PhD from the University of Cambridge.

And what was Elizabeth's ground-breaking discovery? That by keeping the ends of our chromosomes - called telomeres - healthy, humans could potentially prevent diseases and even slow ageing altogether.
A revolutionary discovery!

Shoelace science

If you imagine your chromosomes as shoelaces, the telomeres are the little plastic tips at each end. They protect the shoelace and stop the threads from unravelling.

During our lives, telomeres wear down until they are unable to protect the chromosome properly. It is for this reason that cells lose the ability to repair themselves. And what does that mean?

You got it. **Ageing.**

We all do things that speed up or slow down the breakdown of our telomeres. To try and stop the shortening, we must improve our lifestyle. That means eating well, exercising, getting enough sleep and managing stress. So maybe meditation – used to keep us stress-free – can help protect our telomeres!

Animal ages

Biologists are studying animals with different lifespans to help humans understand how organisms age. Let's look at how long some of these incredible animals can live!

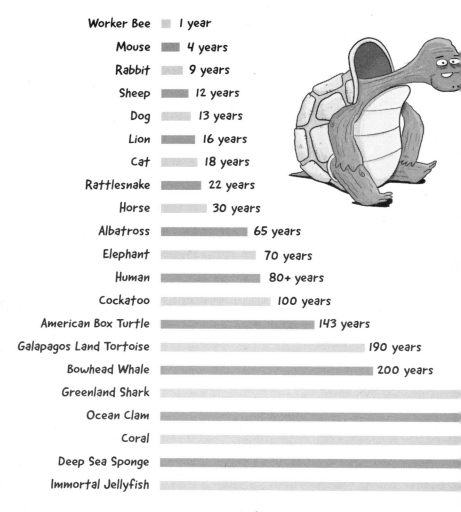

Worker Bee	1 year
Mouse	4 years
Rabbit	9 years
Sheep	12 years
Dog	13 years
Lion	16 years
Cat	18 years
Rattlesnake	22 years
Horse	30 years
Albatross	65 years
Elephant	70 years
Human	80+ years
Cockatoo	100 years
American Box Turtle	143 years
Galapagos Land Tortoise	190 years
Bowhead Whale	200 years
Greenland Shark	
Ocean Clam	
Coral	
Deep Sea Sponge	
Immortal Jellyfish	

400 years

500 years

Now we jump forward a few thousand years!

4000 years

11,000 years!

169

IMMORTAL!
(well, sort of...
see page 172!)

How old?

Jonathan, a Seychelles giant tortoise that lives on St. Helena (an island off West Africa) celebrated his 190th birthday in 2022. He's now the oldest tortoise that's ever lived. Hopefully, he'll make it to 200!

Bowhead whales win the prize for the oldest mammal, living over 200 years. Scientists think they understand why they live so long. They analysed the bowhead whale's genome and found they are much better than humans at repairing cell damage, meaning they don't suffer from age-related diseases as much. Incredible!

Plants aplenty

Some of the oldest organisms on Earth are plants. They can live for thousands of years because they do not grow or reproduce as quickly as most animals do. Scientists found that this could be due to stem cells!

Sea sponges are simple aquatic animals and can live for thousands of years. One research study discovered a deep-sea sponge (*Monorhaphis chuni*) that is over 11,000 years old!

Immortal jellyfish

Researchers have discovered an 'immortal' species of jellyfish that can reverse its ageing process. This incredible organism may hold the key to understanding human ageing and help us develop age-busting medicines.

After their eggs hatch, most jellyfish begin their lives as drifting larvae. They then attach to the seafloor forming a 'polyp' where they bud to form new polyps. Once they mature, they break away and turn into the familiar looking jellyfish.

But one species - *Turritopsis dohrnii* - does something unique. If it's under threat or experiences an injury, it can turn back time and move to the seafloor, returning to its pre-jellyfish polyp state. In time, it can return to the jellyfish stage again as a completely newly formed - and young - organism!

Scientists have discovered that this remarkable jellyfish has many genes associated with DNA repair and it also has mutations that keep its telomeres from breaking down. One day this amazing organism will help us understand how to stop ageing - and possibly even reverse it!

That means you'll get younger rather than older, so you'll have to stay in school **FOREVER**. On second thoughts, let's give that a miss, shall we?

There are other ways we could use technology to 'live forever'...

Cool cryonics

Some people who died from untreatable cancer and other serious diseases are being frozen, in the hope that one day they can be revived!

Before their death, they book themselves a ticket to an incredibly special storage location. After they die, their bodily fluids are drained and replaced with a solution that protects their cells from being damaged by ice crystals.

Next, their bodies are stored permanently in liquid nitrogen at a chilly -196°C. Keeping them at ultra-low temperatures means their bodies are preserved – something known as cryonics.

As well as storing frozen people, there are also plans to store tissues, cells and even the DNA of animals who may be under threat – kind of like a frozen Noah's Ark! The companies who are providing this unique service are charging a LOT of money to keep the frozen people safe for years to come!

Future science: could we be uploaded to the cloud?

A much cheaper option may be to have a scan of your brain uploaded to the metaverse. While your body will age and eventually die, your digital twin will stay young forever, living with virtual copies of your family and friends in cyberspace!

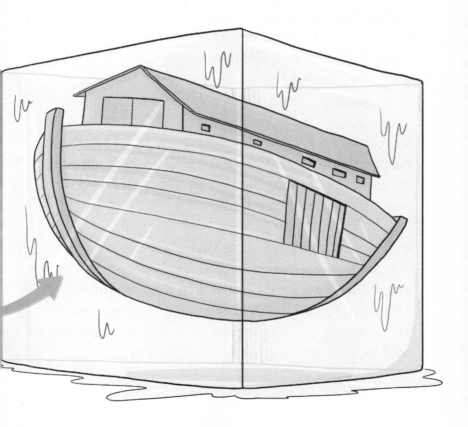

Imagination station

Imagine if you could speak with a person far into the future. What would you say to them? What questions would you ask? What things from today would you want to tell them?

You could ask...

O **What is their favourite food?**

O **What do they do for fun?**

O **Do they own a robot?**

Perhaps you could write a letter or draw them a picture?

CHAPTER 11

THE FINAL FRONTIER

SPACE... The final frontier for humanity!
Did you know that our **BODIES** are carefully
ADAPTED for living on Planet Earth?

In space, it's different. The body has a lot to deal
with! There's no oxygen to breathe, there's low
or no gravity, you're exposed to radiation, and
it can be below **FREEZING**. That means in the
future, if humans move into space, medicine will
need to be adapted to deal with these
new challenges.

It's so important that a whole new science has
been created. It's called **SPACE MEDICINE!**

Space medicine

We take some essential parts of life for granted, such as gravity (which keeps your feet on the ground), clean air to breathe, and sunlight. But when humans leave our planet in a rocket (or by flying saucer if they're kidnapped by aliens), humans suddenly realise how important these essential parts of life really are... and what being without them means. That's why space agencies have whole departments dedicated to space medicine to keep astronauts healthy!

Astronaut health is a top priority. That's because there are lots of hazards in space to deal with. But the amazing thing is... the science we learn in space also helps humans on Earth too. It all adds to the knowledge we have about our health.

Suit up!

Spacesuits are equipped to deal with some of the challenges that space throws at astronauts. The suits have several layers to protect the astronaut from radiation. They also supply oxygen and recycle water from pee and sweat! The visor inside the astronaut's helmet protects their eyes from bright sunlight and the suit keeps the astronaut at just the right temperature.

Space terrors!

Thinking of taking a trip into space? You'll have to contend with all these body-bashing conditions...

RADIATION: high levels can cause burns and permanent damage to our DNA.

LACK OF OXYGEN: there's no air to breathe in space.

SLEEP DISTURBANCE: without our usual sunrises and sunsets, astronauts' sleep patterns can become all messed up!

TEMPERATURE: space is too hot in some places, and absolutely FREEZING in others.

Space doctors

If humans are going to live amongst the stars, scientists and doctors need to come up with new ways to keep us safe! Medical doctors, researchers, psychologists, biomedical engineers and exercise physiologists all play vital roles in looking after astronauts during every stage of a mission.

When did this start?

Space medicine has been around since the 1960s. On April 12, 1961, Yuri Gagarin, a Soviet cosmonaut, became the first human in space. He orbited the Earth aboard his spacecraft, the Vostok 1, before returning safely to Earth. A lot of work was done before Yuri's flight to make sure he stayed healthy.

Space surgery

A robot surgeon called Mira has joined the crew of the International Space Station! In space, robot surgeons will be commonplace. That's because robots may possibly be quicker and more efficient than humans. Robotastic!

And now?

Space medicine is developing at rocket speed! Millions of miles into space and not a hospital in sight, space doctors will need to keep their wits about them. They'll need...

O Devices to perform surgery.

O Robot helpers trained to perform medical procedures.

O Artificial Intelligence to diagnose and even treat illness.

O Telemedicine to consult with scientists and experts back on Earth.

O Virtual Reality for astronauts to socialise, helping them feel less isolated.

Weightless worries

Weightlessness, caused by a lack of gravity, affects the human body in several ways...

- O Muscles and bones start to get weaker.
- O A decrease in blood volume means that astronauts can feel lightheaded.
- O An alteration of a person's senses means astronauts can feel dizzy.

But wait... what is gravity?

It's an invisible force that pulls objects towards each other. The larger the object, the more gravity it has. Earth is so big it pulls us towards the surface, keeping our feet on the ground.

The further people move away, like when they go into space, the less pull there is. This is why astronauts experience weightlessness in space.

Losing your limbs

On Earth, we always know where our body parts are. Our brains have a clever way of working out where everything is. Try closing your eyes and touching your nose. Yes! You can immediately find your nose, can't you? That makes you simply amazing, as every human is.

In space, low gravity means that this ability to sense the body and how it moves doesn't work as well. Astronauts can bump their arms or heads, causing an injury.

What's the answer?

Balance and movement exercises. To help the body learn and adapt to the lack of gravity.

Astronauts on the International Space Station work out using treadmills and exercise bikes for about two hours every single day! This keeps their bodies active and helps them adjust to the sensory changes they may feel from being in space.

Mission to Mars

Space missions will take a long time. People may get sick. Hopefully, many diseases will have been eradicated by the time humans move into space but diagnosing and treating disease will still be part of future space missions.

Martian Medicines

When humans land on Mars, they'll need to take a lot of supplies with them, including oxygen, food and medicine.

With current rocket designs, it will take around nine months to reach Mars. Astronauts would need to be prepared for two-year missions, considering the long trip there and back.

But eventually their supplies will run out. That means they'll need to make more of what they need while they're actually on Mars.

The astropharmacy

Researchers at NASA's Ames Research Center have designed an 'astropharmacy', which will enable future Mars explorers to create medicine on demand. The Astropharmacy is basically a mini laboratory that uses genetically engineered cells to create proteins that can be used to make medicines! Awesome!

Space slumber

Hibernation and sleep are different. Hibernation is when animals like bears and hedgehogs become inactive to save energy during the winter months. Their breathing and heart rate slow, and their body temperature falls.

Although humans can't hibernate, scientific research shows that humans may still hold the genes that could allow us to do so.

Reactivating these genes using gene therapy or genetic modification could help treat disease and let us live much longer lives.

Hibernation information

O Most squirrels don't hold enough body fat to hibernate. Instead, they hide food around the forest. Then, in winter, they sleep for most of the day but head out at sunrise for a quick morning snack, eating from their secret stash of grub!

O In winter, some snails retract inside their shell and seal the exit with slime, then don't emerge until spring!

It may also allow humans to travel deep in space, as we could hibernate for many decades at a time. Learning to reactivate a human's ability to hibernate would be like harnessing an incredible superpower!

Alien attack!

What happens if we do make it to other worlds? You guessed it: we'll face even more health challenges!

The scariest thing? No, it's not mega monsters or killer robots.

We could come under attack from **ALIEN MICRO-ORGANISMS!**

OK, that's a little dramatic. They may not exactly 'attack', but they could potentially cause health problems. We've seen with COVID-19 how a new virus on Earth can cause havoc.

Extraterrestrial microorganisms (such as bacteria, viruses, parasites and fungi) could be so different that our immune systems wouldn't stand a chance...

And what if alien microbes were accidently brought back? All it takes is for an astronaut to step in the wrong place and they could bring something truly terrible back on the bottom of their boot!

But don't worry - this is unlikely to happen for a very long time. If at all!

Creation station

URGENT! You need to design a space ambulance to take the injured from the Martian surface to their orbiting space station.

Would it be more like a plane or rocket? Or can you think of a completely new design?

Draw a picture and don't forget to add flashing lights, so everyone knows it's an ambulance!

CHAPTER 12

FUTURE
FANTASTIC

As scientists develop new medicines and find
new treatments, others will learn from their
achievements and be inspired to make their own
medical breakthroughs in the future.

Science builds on science. Every great
innovation comes from a single idea: a **SPARK**
inside someone's **IMAGINATION**.

Innovators ask questions such as "What if?"
And **QUESTIONS** need **ANSWERS**.

So, what does our future hold? Can you
imagine?

Fantastic futurology

Some scientists analyse past and present events and trends, in the hope of predicting future events. These people are called **futurists**.

Futurists try to predict what is likely to continue and what could possibly change.

They look at advancements that are:

O scientific
O social
O technological

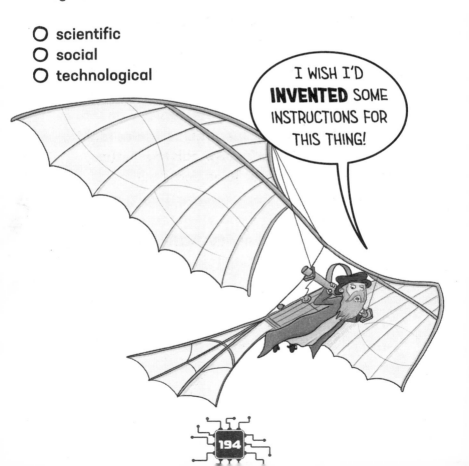

Changing the world... one idea at a time

Some of the greatest thinkers are not only scientists but also artists, writers, inventors or other creatives.

The imagination is our greatest tool!

Fantastic futurists

O The Renaissance artist Leonardo da Vinci drew sketches of ornithopters - machines that fly by flapping their wings!

O Technology such as submarines, space flight and solar panels were all predicted by the science fiction writer Jules Verne over 150 years ago!

O The 19th-century American writer Mark Twain wrote a story predicting television in 1898. Clever!

Amazing Arthur

In 1970, the famous physicist, futurist and sci-fi author, Arthur C Clarke said:

Although Arthur wrote his novels and essays many years ago, he managed to correctly predict several scientific and technological breakthroughs.

Here are some of Arthur's incredibly accurate visions of the future:

O In 1945 Arthur wrote that 'artificial satellites' would remain above the Earth in the same spot, helping build a communications network. Geosynchronous satellites didn't happen until 1963!

O In 1964, Arthur said 'it will be possible for a man to conduct his business from Tahiti or Bali just as well as he could from London.' Arthur had predicted remote working!

O In 1974 Arthur described how people would use 'a console at home' where you could get all the information you need for everyday life, from bank statements to theatre reservations. It sounds like Arthur predicted both the smartphone and internet!

Arthur was an incredible futurist. He showed us all a basic sum to change the world:

IMAGINATION + SCIENCE + TECHNOLOGY + ENGINEERING + MATHS = THE FUTURE

Don't go bacon my heart

Meet Malorie Blackman, another fabulous futurist. In the 1990s, Malorie read an article about how we'd need to implant animal organs to deal with the lack of human donors. The scientific term for this is xenotransplantation (see page 88).

That's a tough word - you say it like this:

Zeh-no-trans-plant-ay-shun.

QUESTIONS ARE ONE OF THE BEST PLACES TO START FROM WHEN **WRITING** A NOVEL.

Author
Malorie Blackman

Malorie was so fascinated by the idea that she wrote a story about a boy with a serious heart condition who ended up having a pig's heart transplanted into him. Her book, Pig-Heart Boy, was published in 1997. At the time, it was known that for xenotransplantation to work, human DNA would need to be added to the animal embryos, to reduce the chance of organ rejection. This is known as gene editing.

In 2022, this fantastical idea became reality when David Bennett in the USA received a pig heart transplant. To make sure the new heart was not rejected, scientists had to alter ten different genes in the donor pig. Unfortunately, David passed away two months after this ground-breaking surgery. But he will go down in history thanks to this incredible medical milestone.

And so will Malorie, who imagined it way ahead of time!

Medical marvel or made up?

A lot of science is so incredible, it feels like something from the future. It's not always easy to tell the difference between record-breaking science fact and science fiction.

Can you work out which of the below medical marvels are real and which are made up?

Two beagles were cloned from skin cells and edited using CRISPR to be the first gene-edited dogs in the world.

Paralysed mice walked again after a single injection of stem cells.

Scientists are mapping the DNA of every living creature in the whole of the British Isles.

An AI called Deep Mind predicted the structure of all known proteins known to science in less than eighteen months.

Pig organs were partially revived hours after the pig's death.

A poo-like slime robot was built that can clean your insides as it moves through your gorgeous guts.

MUST CLEAN GUTS!!

Turn the page upside down to see the answers!

A: They're all real medical marvels!

AI apocalypse

Lots of people think that artificially intelligent computers will **take over the world**. The famous physicist Professor Stephen Hawking even warned about it! He said...

The development of full artificial intelligence could spell the end of the human race!

Stephen appreciated that early forms of AI were helping humanity in many ways. But he feared what could happen in the future if we created something that might be cleverer than us!

If AI is more intelligent, could it take over and get rid of humans? Possibly. But on the other hand, AI could **SAVE** humanity, by helping to eradicate disease and poverty and even averting climate change!

For example, in 2022 an AI called ESMFold was able to predict the shape of over 600 million proteins in viruses, bacteria and other microbes. If that's not amazing enough, the AI did it in less than 2 weeks. This will speed up drug discovery in incredible ways!

Gene juggle

By changing genes - using gene therapy, genetic modification or gene editing - it's possible that all genetic diseases could be eliminated. This is fantastic, but there are risks too...

As science and medicine develop, we must keep a check on how we use these incredible technologies. **Just because we can do something, doesn't mean we should.**

Zombie hamsters

Scientists and doctors must consider all the positives and negatives of using new technologies in different ways. This is called ethics. Ethics applies to many things, but it's very important in medicine.

Why do we have ethics? Well, we need to keep a check on things, because sometimes things can go wrong...

For example, scientists in the US did a gene-editing experiment and accidentally created super aggressive **MUTANT HAMSTERS!**

Researchers were studying a hormone called vasopressin. Using gene editing, they changed the way the hormone was used by hamsters, hoping that it would make them more social. But the hamsters became **SUPER AGGRESSIVE** and attacked each other, almost as though they were zombies.

So we need to be very careful with all this new technology. We don't want to end up becoming zombies!

Back in time?

The future of medicine is exciting, but things may not progress as we would hope. We could quite easily go backwards if we're not careful!

Antibiotics - medicines that kill bacteria or prevent them from spreading - paved the way for fantastic future medicine.

But many people are getting sick and dying around the world because antibiotics are no longer working. The microbes are gaining resistance. This means that they can't be killed off as easily.

Without antibiotics, modern medicine will cease to exist. Patients with cancer on chemotherapy need them to fight infections. Medical procedures or surgeries can't go ahead without them to prevent infection.

Packed planet

Eliminating all diseases sounds like an honourable thing to do. But it would make new problems for humanity to solve, and the biggest problem of all? There won't be enough resources or space. We'll end up with a packed planet!

So maybe we could expand our civilisation to the stars! We could live in space stations, on the moon, or on other planets like Mars. It could be the start of a galactic empire! Hopefully not like Darth Vader's Empire. More like the Federation of Planets in Star Trek. Much friendlier.

Come to think of it, Darth Vader was a cyborg. As we change and enhance our bodies, augmenting them with technology, will we still be human?

There are so many questions for future scientists to answer. And best of all - **YOU** could be the one answering them!

Future fantastic

Can you imagine details of future science? Maybe some of your predictions will come true!

Perhaps in the future, people will be cyborgs with bionic limbs and nanobots in their blood. Or maybe they'll be pretty much the same as we are today!

The future's bright. But to be honest, none of us can be sure what the future holds.

But there's one thing we do know.

It's **YOU**, our future scientists, doctors, innovators and creatives who will create the future for our health.

So go ahead, and make it happen. Future humans are counting on you!